THE HOLY GOSPEL OF JESUS CHRIST
ACCORDING TO SAINT MATTHEW

THE HOLY GOSPEL OF JESUS CHRIST ACCORDING TO SAINT MATTHEW

Based on Douay-Rheims, catholic Bible.

ISBN: 978-1-963956-26-9

Contents

tribute to be paid to Caesar. He confutes the Sadducees, shews which is the first commandment in the law and puzzles the Pharisees.

Saint Matthew, one of the twelve Apostles, who from being a publican, that is, a tax gatherer, was called by our Saviour to the Apostleship: in that profession his name is Levi. (Luke 5.27, and Mark 2.14.) He was the first of the Evangelists that wrote the Gospel, and that in Hebrew or Syro-Chaldaic which the Jews in Palestine spoke at that time. The original is not now extant; but it was translated in the time of the Apostles into Greek, that version was of equal authority. He wrote about six years after the Lord's Ascension.

Chapter 1

The genealogy of Christ: he is conceived and born of a virgin.

1:1. The book of the generation of Jesus Christ, the son of David, the son of Abraham:

1:2. Abraham begot Isaac. And Isaac begot Jacob. And Jacob begot Judas and his brethren.

1:3. And Judas begot Phares and Zara of Thamar. And Phares begot Esron. And Esron begot Aram.

1:4. And Aram begot Aminadab. And Aminadab begot Naasson. And Naasson begot Salmon.

1:5. And Salmon begot Booz of Rahab. And Booz begot Obed of Ruth. And Obed begot Jesse.

1:6. And Jesse begot David the king. And David

the king begot Solomon, of her that had been the wife of Urias.

1:7. And Solomon begot Roboam. And Roboam begot Abia. And Abia begot Asa.

1:8. And Asa begot Josaphat. And Josaphat begot Joram. And Joram begot Ozias.

1:9. And Ozias begot Joatham. And Joatham begot Achaz. And Achaz begot Ezechias.

1:10. And Ezechias begot Manasses. And Manasses begot Amon. And Amon begot Josias.

1:11. And Josias begot Jechonias and his brethren in the transmigration of Babylon.

1:12. And after the transmigration of Babylon, Jechonias begot Salathiel. And Salathiel begot Zorobabel.

1:13. And Zorobabel begot Abiud. And Abiud begot Eliacim. And Eliacim begot Azor.

1:14. And Azor begot Sadoc. And Sadoc begot Achim. And Achim begot Eliud.

1:15. And Eliud begot Eleazar. And Eleazar begot Mathan. And Mathan begot Jacob.

1:16. And Jacob begot Joseph the husband of Mary, of whom was born Jesus, who is called Christ.

The husband of Mary... The Evangelist gives us rather the pedigree of St. Joseph, than that of the blessed Virgin, to conform to the custom of the Hebrews, who in their genealogies took no notice of women; but as they were near akin, the pedigree of the one sheweth that of the other.

1:17. So all the generations from Abraham to David, are fourteen generations. And from David to the transmigration of Babylon, are fourteen generations: and from the transmigration of Babylon to Christ are fourteen generations.

1:18. Now the generation of Christ was in this wise. When as his mother Mary was espoused to Joseph, before they came together, she was found with child, of the Holy Ghost.

1:19. Whereupon Joseph her husband, being a just man, and not willing publicly to expose her, was minded to put her away privately.

1:20. But while he thought on these things, behold the Angel of the Lord appeared to him in his sleep, saying: Joseph, son of David, fear not to take unto thee Mary thy wife, for that which is conceived in her, is of the Holy Ghost.

1:21. And she shall bring forth a son: and thou shalt call his name Jesus. For he shall save his people from their sins.

1:22. Now all this was done that it might be fulfilled which the Lord spoke by the prophet, saying:

1:23. Behold a virgin shall be with child, and bring forth a son, and they shall call his name Emmanuel, which being interpreted is, God with us.

1:24. And Joseph rising up from sleep, did as the angel of the Lord had commanded him, and took unto him his wife.

1:25. And he knew her not till she brought forth her first born son: and he called his name Jesus.

Till she brought forth her firstborn son... From these words Helvidius and other heretics most impiously inferred that the blessed Virgin Mary had other children besides Christ; but St. Jerome shews, by divers examples, that this expression of the Evangelist was a manner of speaking usual among the Hebrews, to denote by the word until, only what is done, without any regard to the future.

Thus it is said, Genesis 8. 6 and 7, that Noe sent forth a raven, which went forth, and did not return till the waters were dried up on the earth. That is, did not return any more. Also Isaias 46. 4, God says: I am till you grow old. Who dare infer that God should then cease to be: Also in the first book of Machabees 5. 54, And they went up to mount Sion with joy and gladness, and offered holocausts, because not one of them was slain till they had returned in peace. That is, not one was slain before or after they had returned.

God saith to his divine Son: Sit on my right hand till I make thy enemies thy footstool. Shall he sit no longer after his enemies are subdued? Yea and for all eternity. St. Jerome also proves by

Scripture examples, that an only begotten son, was also called firstborn, or first begotten: because according to the law, the firstborn males were to be consecrated to God; Sanctify unto me, saith the Lord, every firstborn that openeth the womb among the children of Israel, etc. Ex. 13. 2.

Chapter 2

The offerings of the wise men: the flight into Egypt: the massacre of the Innocents.

2:1. When Jesus therefore was born in Bethlehem of Juda, in the days of king Herod, behold, there came wise men from the East to Jerusalem,

2:2. Saying: Where is he that is born king of the Jews? For we have seen his star in the East, and are come to adore him.

2:3. And king Herod hearing this, was troubled, and all Jerusalem with him.

2:4. And assembling together all the chief priests and the scribes of the people, he inquired of them where Christ should be born.

2:5. But they said to him: In Bethlehem of Juda. For so it is written by the prophet:

2:6. And thou Bethlehem the land of Juda art not the least among the princes of Juda: for out of thee shall come forth the captain that shall rule my people Israel.

2:7. Then Herod, privately calling the wise men learned diligently of them the time of the star which appeared to them;

2:8. And sending them into Bethlehem, said: Go and diligently inquire after the child, and when you have found him, bring me word again, that I also may come and adore him.

2:9. Who having heard the king, went their way; and behold the star which they had seen in the East, went before them, until it came and stood over where the child was.

2:10. And seeing the star they rejoiced with exceeding great joy.

2:11. And entering into the house, they found the child with Mary his mother, and falling down they adored him: and opening their treasures, they offered him gifts; gold, frankincense, and myrrh.

2:12. And having received an answer in sleep that they should not return to Herod, they went back another way into their country.

2:13. And after they were departed, behold an angel of the Lord appeared in sleep to Joseph, saying: Arise, and take the child and his mother, and fly into Egypt: and be there until I shall tell thee. For it will come to pass that Herod will seek the child to destroy him.

2:14. Who arose, and took the child and his

mother by night, and retired into Egypt: and he was there until the death of Herod:

2:15. That it might be fulfilled which the Lord spoke by the prophet, saying: Out of Egypt have I called my son.

2:16. Then Herod perceiving that he was deluded by the wise men, was exceeding angry: and sending killed all the men children that were in Bethlehem, and in all the borders thereof, from two years old and under, according to the time which he had diligently inquired of the wise men.

2:17. Then was fulfilled that which was spoken by Jeremias the prophet, saying:

2:18. A voice in Rama was heard, lamentation and great mourning; Rachel bewailing her children, and would not be comforted, because they are not.

2:19. But when Herod was dead, behold an angel of the Lord appeared in sleep to Joseph in Egypt,

2:20. Saying: Arise, and take the child and his mother, and go into the land of Israel. For they are dead that sought the life of the child.

2:21. Who arose, and took the child and his mother, and came into the land of Israel.

2:22. But hearing that Archclaus reigned in Judea in the room of Herod his father, he was afraid to go thither: and being warned in sleep retired into the quarters of Galilee.

2:23. And coming he dwelt in a city called Nazareth: that it might be fulfilled which was said by the prophets: That he shall be called a Nazarene.

Chapter 3

The preaching of John: Christ is baptized.

3:1. And in those days cometh John the Baptist preaching in the desert of Judea.

3:2. And saying: Do penance: for the kingdom of heaven is at hand.

Do penance... Paenitentiam agite. Which word, according to the use of the scriptures and the holy fathers, does not only signify repentance and amendment of life, but also punishing past sins by fasting, and such like penitential exercises.

3:3. For this is he that was spoken of by Isaias the prophet, saying: A voice of one crying in the desert, Prepare ye the way of the Lord, make straight his paths.

3:4. And the same John had his garment of camel's hair, and a leathern girdle about his loins: and his meat was locusts and wild honey.

3:5. Then went out to him Jerusalem and all Judea, and all the country about Jordan:

3:6. And were baptized by him in the Jordan, confessing their sins.

3:7. And seeing many of the Pharisees and Sadducees coming to his baptism, he said to them: Ye brood of vipers, who hath shewed you to flee from the wrath to come?

Pharisees and Sadducees... These were two sects among the Jews: of which the former were for the most part notorious hypocrites; the latter, a kind of freethinkers in matters of religion.

3:8. Bring forth therefore fruit worthy of penance.

3:9. And think not to say within yourselves, We have Abraham for our father. For I tell you that God is able of these stones to raise up children to Abraham.

3:10. For now the axe is laid to the root of the trees. Every tree therefore that doth not yield good fruit, shall be cut down, and cast into the fire.

3:11. I indeed baptize you in water unto penance, but he that shall come after me, is mightier than I, whose shoes I am not worthy to bear: he shall baptize you in the Holy Ghost and fire.

3:12. Whose fan is in his hand, and he will thoroughly cleanse his floor and gather his wheat into the barn; but the chaff he will burn with unquenchable fire.

3:13. Then cometh Jesus from Galilee to the Jordan, unto John, to be baptized by him.

3:14. But John stayed him, saying: I ought to be baptized by thee, and comest thou to me?

3:15. And Jesus answering, said to him: Suffer it to be so now. For so it becometh us to fulfil all justice. Then he suffered him.

3:16. And Jesus being baptized, forthwith came out of the water: and lo, the heavens were opened to him: and he saw the Spirit of God descending as a dove, and coming upon him.

3:17. And behold a voice from heaven saying: This is my beloved Son, in whom I am well pleased.

Chapter 4

Christ's fast of forty days: He is tempted. He begins to preach, to call disciples to him, and to work miracles.

4:1. Then Jesus was led by the spirit into the desert, to be tempted by the devil.

4:2. And when he had fasted forty days and forty nights, afterwards he was hungry.

4:3. And the tempter coming said to him: If thou be the Son of God, command that these stones be made bread.

4:4. Who answered and said: It is written, Not

in bread alone doth man live, but in every word that proceedeth from the mouth of God.

4:5. Then the devil took him up into the holy city, and set him upon the pinnacle of the temple,

4:6. And said to him: If thou be the Son of God, cast thyself down, for it is written: That he hath given his angels charge over thee, and in their hands shall they bear thee up, lest perhaps thou dash thy foot against a stone.

4:7. Jesus said to him: It is written again: Thou shalt not tempt the Lord thy God.

4:8. Again the devil took him up into a very high mountain, and shewed him all the kingdoms of the world, and the glory of them,

Shewed him, etc... That is, pointed out to him where each kingdom lay; and set forth in words what was most glorious and admirable in each of them. Or also set before his eyes, as it were in a large map, a lively representation of all those kingdoms.

4:9. And said to him: All these will I give thee, if falling down thou wilt adore me.

4:10. Then Jesus saith to him: Begone, Satan: for it is written: The Lord thy God shalt thou adore, and him only shalt thou serve.

4:11. Then the devil left him; and behold angels came and ministered to him.

4:12. And when Jesus had heard that John was delivered up, he retired into Galilee:

4:13. And leaving the city Nazareth, he came and dwelt in Capharnaum on the sea coast, in the borders of Zabulon and of Nephthalim;

4:14. That it might be fulfilled which was said by Isaias the prophet:

4:15. Land of Zabulon and land of Nephthalim, the way of the sea beyond the Jordan, Galilee of the Gentiles:

4:16. The people that sat in darkness, hath seen great light: and to them that sat in the region of the shadow of death, light is sprung up.

4:17. From that time Jesus began to preach, and to say: Do penance, for the kingdom of heaven is at hand.

4:18. And Jesus walking by the sea of Galilee, saw two brethren, Simon who is called Peter, and Andrew his brother, casting a net into the sea (for they were fishers).

4:19. And he saith to them: Come ye after me, and I will make you to be fishers of men.

4:20. And they immediately leaving their nets, followed him.

4:21. And going on from thence, he saw other

two brethren, James the son of Zebedee, and John his brother, in a ship with Zebedee their father, mending their nets: and he called them.

4:22. And they forthwith left their nets and father, and followed him.

4:23. And Jesus went about all Galilee, teaching in their synagogues, and preaching the gospel of the kingdom: and healing all manner of sickness and every infirmity, among the people.

4:24. And his fame went throughout all Syria, and they presented to him all sick people that were taken with divers diseases and torments, and such as were possessed by devils, and lunatics, and those that had the palsy, and he cured them:

4:25. And much people followed him from Galilee, and from Decapolis, and from Jerusalem, and from Judea, and from beyond the Jordan.

Chapter 5

Christ's sermon upon the mount. The eight beatitudes.

5:1. And seeing the multitudes, he went up into a mountain, and when he was set down, his disciples came unto him.

5:2. And opening his mouth he taught them, saying:

5:3. Blessed are the poor in spirit: for theirs is

the kingdom of heaven.

The poor in spirit... That is, the humble; and they whose spirit is not set upon riches.

5:4. Blessed are the meek: for they shall possess the land.

5:5. Blessed are they that mourn: for they shall be comforted.

5:6. Blessed are they that hunger and thirst after justice: for they shall have their fill.

5:7. Blessed are the merciful: for they shall obtain mercy.

5:8. Blessed are the clean of heart: they shall see God.

5:9. Blessed are the peacemakers: for they shall be called the children of God.

5:10. Blessed are they that suffer persecution for justice' sake: for theirs is the kingdom of heaven.

5:11. Blessed are ye when they shall revile you, and persecute you, and speak all that is evil against you, untruly, for my sake:

5:12. Be glad and rejoice for your reward is very great in heaven. For so they persecuted the prophets that were before you.

5:13. You are the salt of the earth. But if the salt

lose its savour, wherewith shall it be salted? It is good for nothing anymore but to be cast out, and to be trodden on by men.

5:14. You are the light of the world. A city seated on a mountain cannot be hid.

5:15. Neither do men light a candle and put it under a bushel, but upon a candlestick, that it may shine to all that are in the house.

5:16. So let your light shine before men, that they may see your good works, and glorify your Father who is in heaven.

5:17. Do not think that I am come to destroy the law, or the prophets. I am not come to destroy, but to fulfil.

To fulfil... By accomplishing all the figures and prophecies; and perfecting all that was imperfect.

5:18. For amen I say unto you, till heaven and earth pass, one jot, or one tittle shall not pass of the law, till all be fulfilled.

Amen... That is, assuredly of a truth... This Hebrew word, amen, is here retained by the example and authority of all the four Evangelists. It is used by our Lord as a strong asseveration, and affirmation of the truth.

5:19. He therefore that shall break one of these least commandments, and shall so teach men shall be called the least in the kingdom of heaven. But he that shall do and teach, he shall be called great in the kingdom of heaven.

5:20. For I tell you, that unless your justice abound more than that of the scribes and Pharisees, you shall not enter into the kingdom of heaven.

The scribes and Pharisees... The scribes were the doctors of the law of Moses: the Pharisees were a precise set of men, making profession of a more exact observance of the law: and upon that account greatly esteemed among the people.

5:21. You have heard that it was said to them of old: Thou shalt not kill. And whosoever shall kill, shall be in danger of the judgment.

Shall be in danger of the judgment... That is, shall deserve to be punished by that lesser tribunal among the Jews, called the Judgment, which took cognizance of such crimes.

5:22. But I say to you, that whosoever is angry with his brother, shall be in danger of the judgment. And whosoever shall say to his brother, Raca, shall be in danger of the council. And whosoever shall say, Thou fool, shall be in danger of hell fire.

Raca... A word expressing great indignation or contempt. Shall be in danger of the council... That is, shall deserve to be punished by the highest court of judicature, called the Council, or Sanhedrim, consisting of seventy-two persons, where the highest causes were tried and judged, which was at Jerusalem. Thou fool... This was then looked upon as a heinous injury, when uttered with contempt, spite, or malice: and therefore is here so severely condemned. Shall be in danger of hell fire... literally, according to the Greek, shall deserve to be cast into the Gehenna of fire. Which words our Saviour made use of to express the fire and punishments of hell.

5:23. If therefore thou offer thy gift at the altar, and there thou remember that thy brother hath anything against thee;

5:24. Leave there thy offering before the altar, and go first to be reconciled to thy brother, and then coming thou shalt offer thy gift.

5:25. Be at agreement with thy adversary betimes, whilst thou art in the way with him: lest perhaps the adversary deliver thee to the judge, and the judge deliver thee to the officer, and thou be cast into prison.

5:26. Amen I say to thee, thou shalt not go out from thence till thou repay the last farthing.

5:27. You have heard that it was said to them of old: Thou shalt not commit adultery.

5:28. But I say to you, that whosoever shall look on a woman to lust after her, hath already committed adultery with her in his heart.

5:29. And if thy right eye scandalize thee, pluck

it out and cast it from thee. For it is expedient for thee that one of thy members should perish, rather than thy whole body be cast into hell.

Scandalize thee... That is, if it be a stumbling-block, or occasion of sin to thee. By which we are taught to fly the immediate occasions of sin, though they be as dear to us, or as necessary as a hand or an eye.

5:30. And if thy right hand scandalize thee, cut it off, and cast it from thee: for it is expedient for thee that one of thy members should perish, rather than that thy whole body go into hell.

5:31. And it hath been said, Whosoever shall put away his wife, let him give her a bill of divorce.

5:32. But I say to you, that whosoever shall put away his wife, excepting the cause of fornication, maketh her to commit adultery: and he that shall marry her that is put away, committeth adultery.

5:33. Again you have heard that it was said to them of old, thou shalt not forswear thyself: but thou shalt perform thy oaths to the Lord.

5:34. But I say to you not to swear at all, neither by heaven for it is the throne of God:

Not to swear at all... It is not forbid to swear in truth, justice and judgment; to the honour of God, or our own or neighbour's just defence: but only to swear rashly, or profanely, in common discourse, and without necessity.

5:35. Nor by the earth, for it is his footstool: nor by Jerusalem, for it is the city of the great king:

5:36. Neither shalt thou swear by thy head, because thou canst not make one hair white or black.

5:37. But let your speech be yea, yea: no, no: and that which is over and above these, is of evil.

5:38. You have heard that it hath been said: An eye for an eye, and a tooth for a tooth.

5:39. But I say to you not to resist evil: but if one strike thee on thy right cheek, turn to him also the other:

Not to resist evil, etc... What is here commanded, is a Christian patience under injuries and affronts, and to be willing even to suffer still more, rather than to indulge the desire of revenge: but what is further added does not strictly oblige according to the letter, for neither did Christ nor St. Paul turn the other cheek. St. John 18., and Acts 23.

5:40. And if a man will contend with thee in judgment, and take away thy coat, let go thy cloak also unto him.

5:41. And whosoever will force thee one mile, go with him other two.

5:42. Give to him that asketh of thee, and from him that would borrow of thee turn not away.

5:43. You have heard that it hath been said, Thou shalt love thy neighbour, and hate thy enemy.

5:44. But I say to you, Love your enemies: do good to them that hate you: and pray for them that persecute and calumniate you:

5:45. That you may be the children of your Father who is in heaven, who maketh his sun to rise upon the good, and bad, and raineth upon the just and the unjust.

5:46. For if you love them that love you, what reward shall you have? do not even the publicans this?

The publicans... These were the gatherers of the public taxes: a set of men, odious and infamous among the Jews, for their extortions and injustice.

5:47. And if you salute your brethren only, what do you more? do not also the heathens this?

5:48. Be you therefore perfect, as also your heavenly Father is perfect.

Chapter 6

A continuation of the sermon on the mount.

6:1. Take heed that you do not your justice before men, to be seen by them: otherwise you shall not have a reward of your Father who is in heaven.

Your justice... that is, works of justice; viz., fasting, prayer, and almsdeeds; which ought to be performed not out of ostentation, or a view to please men, but solely to please God.

6:2. Therefore when thou dost an alms-deed, sound not a trumpet before thee, as the hypocrites do in the synagogues and in the streets, that they may be honoured by men. Amen I say to you, they have received their reward.

6:3. But when thou dost alms, let not thy left hand know what thy right hand doth.

6:4. That thy alms may be in secret, and thy Father who seeth in secret will repay thee.

6:5. And when ye pray, you shall not be as the hypocrites, that love to stand and pray in the synagogues and corners of the streets, that they may be seen by men: Amen I say to you, they have received their reward.

6:6. But thou when thou shalt pray, enter into thy chamber, and having shut the door, pray to thy Father in secret, and thy father who seeth in secret will repay thee.

6:7. And when you are praying, speak not much, as the heathens. For they think that in their much speaking they may be heard.

6:8. Be not you therefore like to them for your Father knoweth what is needful for you, before you ask him.

6:9. Thus therefore shall you pray: Our Father who art in heaven, hallowed be thy name.

6:10. Thy kingdom come. Thy will be done on earth as it is in heaven.

6:11. Give us this day our supersubstantial bread.

Super substantial bread... In St. Luke the same word is rendered daily bread. It is understood of the bread of life, which we receive in the Blessed Sacrament.

6:12. And forgive us our debts, as we also forgive our debtors.

6:13. And lead us not into temptation. But deliver us from evil. Amen.

Lead us not into temptation... That is, suffer us not to be overcome by temptation.

6:14. For if you will forgive men their offences, your heavenly Father will forgive you also your offences.

6:15. But if you will not forgive men, neither will your Father forgive you your offences.

6:16. And when you fast, be not as the hypocrites, sad. For they disfigure their faces, that they may appear unto men to fast. Amen I say to you, they have received their reward.

6:17. But thou, when thou fastest anoint thy head, and wash thy face;

6:18. That thou appear not to men to fast, but to thy Father who is in secret: and thy Father who seeth in secret, will repay thee.

6:19. Lay not up to yourselves treasures on earth: where the rust, and moth consume, and where thieves break through, and steal.

6:20. But lay up to yourselves treasures in heaven: where neither the rust nor moth doth consume, and where thieves do not break through, nor steal.

6:21. For where thy treasure is, there is thy heart also.

6:22. The light of thy body is thy eye. If thy eye be single, thy whole body shall be lightsome.

6:23. But if thy eye be evil thy whole body shall be darksome. If then the light that is in thee, be darkness: the darkness itself how great shall it be!

6:24. No man can serve two masters. For either he will hate the one, and love the other: or he will sustain the one, and despise the other. You cannot serve God and mammon.

Mammon... That is, riches, worldly interest.

6:25. Therefore I say to you, be not solicitous for your life, what you shall eat, nor for your body, what you shall put on. Is not the life more than the meat: and the body more than the raiment?

6:26. Behold the birds of the air, for they neither sow, nor do they reap, nor gather into barns: and your heavenly Father feedeth them. Are not you of much more value than they?

6:27. And which of you by taking thought, can add to his stature one cubit?

6:28. And for raiment why are you solicitous? Consider the lilies of the field, how they grow: they labour not, neither do they spin.

6:29. But I say to you, that not even Solomon in all his glory was arrayed as one of these.

6:30. And if the grass of the field, which is to day, and to morrow is cast into the oven, God doth so clothe: how much more you, O ye of little faith?

6:31. Be not solicitous therefore, saying: What shall we eat: or what shall we drink, or wherewith shall we be clothed?

6:32. For after all these things do the heathens seek. For your Father knoweth that you have need of all these things.

6:33. Seek ye therefore first the kingdom of God, and his justice, and all these things shall be added unto you.

6:34. Be not therefore solicitous for to morrow; for the morrow will be solicitous for itself. Sufficient for the day is the evil thereof.

Chapter 7

The third part of the sermon on the mount.

7:1. Judge not, that you may not be judged.

7:2. For with what judgment you judge, you shall be judged: and with what measure you mete, it shall be measured to you again.

7:3. And why seest thou the mote that is in thy brother's eye; and seest not the beam that is in thy own eye?

7:4. Or how sayest thou to thy brother: Let me cast the mote out of thy eye; and behold a beam is in thy own eye?

7:5. Thou hypocrite, cast out first the beam out of thy own eye, and then shalt thou see to cast out the mote out of thy brother's eye.

7:6. Give not that which is holy to dogs; neither cast ye your pearls before swine, lest perhaps they trample them under their feet, and turning upon you, they tear you.

7:7. Ask, and it shall be given you: seek, and you shall find: knock, and it shall be opened to you.

7:8. For every one that asketh, receiveth: and he that seeketh, findeth: and to him that knocketh, it shall be opened.

7:9. Or what man is there among you, of whom if his son shall ask bread, will he reach him a stone?

7:10. Or if he shall ask him a fish, will he reach him a serpent?

7:11. If you then being evil, know how to give good gifts to your children: how much more will your Father who is in heaven, give good things to them that ask him?

7:12. All things therefore whatsoever you would that men should do to you, do you also to them. For this is the law and the prophets.

7:13. Enter ye in at the narrow gate: for wide is the gate, and broad is the way that leadeth to destruction, and many there are who go in thereat.

7:14. How narrow is the gate, and strait is the way that leadeth to life: and few there are that find it!

7:15. Beware of false prophets, who come to you in the clothing of sheep, but inwardly they are ravening wolves.

7:16. By their fruits you shall know them. Do men gather grapes of thorns, or figs of thistles?

7:17. Even so every good tree bringeth forth

good fruit, and the evil tree bringeth forth evil
fruit.

7:18. A good tree cannot bring forth evil fruit,
neither can an evil tree bring forth good fruit.

7:19. Every tree that bringeth not forth good
fruit, shall be cut down, and shall be cast into the
fire.

7:20. Wherefore by their fruits you shall know
them.

7:21. Not every one that saith to me, Lord, Lord,
shall enter into the kingdom of heaven: but he that
doth the will of my Father who is in heaven, he
shall enter into the kingdom of heaven.

7:22. Many will say to me in that day: Lord,
Lord, have not we prophesied in thy name, and cast
out devils in thy name, and done many miracles
in thy name?

7:23. And then will I profess unto them, I never
knew you: depart from me, you that work iniquity.

7:24. Every one therefore that heareth these my
words, and doth them, shall be likened to a wise
man that built his house upon a rock,

7:25. And the rain fell, and the floods came, and
the winds blew, and they beat upon that house, and
it fell not, for it was founded on a rock.

7:26. And every one that heareth these my

words and doth them not, shall be like a foolish man that built his house upon the sand,

7:27. And the rain fell, and the floods came, and the winds blew, and they beat upon that house, and it fell, and great was the fall thereof.

7:28. And it came to pass when Jesus had fully ended these words, the people were in admiration at his doctrine.

7:29. For he was teaching them as one having power, and not as the scribes and Pharisees.

Chapter 8

Christ cleanses the leper, heals the centurion's servant, Peter's mother-in-law, and many others: he stills the storm at sea, drives the devils out of two men possessed, and suffers them to go into the swine.

8:1. And when he was come down from the mountain, great multitudes followed him:

8:2. And behold a leper came and adored him, saying: Lord, if thou wilt, thou canst make me clean.

8:3. And Jesus stretching forth his hand, touched him, saying: I will, be thou made clean. And forthwith his leprosy was cleansed.

8:4. And Jesus saith to him: See thou tell no man: but go, shew thyself to the priest, and offer the gift which Moses commanded, for a testimony unto them.

8:5. And when he had entered into Capharnaum, there came to him a centurion, beseeching
him,

8:6. And saying, Lord, my servant lieth at home
sick of the palsy, and is grievously tormented.

8:7. And Jesus saith to him: I will come and
heal him.
8:8. And the centurion, making answer, said:
Lord, I am not worthy that thou shouldst enter
under my roof; but only say the word, and my
servant shall be healed.

8:9. For I also am a man subject to authority,
having under me soldiers; and I say to this, Go, and
he goeth, and to another Come, and he cometh,
and to my servant, Do this, and he doeth it.

8:10. And Jesus hearing this, marvelled; and
said to them that followed him. Amen I say to you,
I have not found so great faith in Israel.

8:11. And I say to you that many shall come
from the east and the west, and shall sit down with
Abraham, and Isaac and Jacob in the kingdom of
heaven:

8:12. But the children of the kingdom shall be
cast out into the exterior darkness: there shall be
weeping and gnashing of teeth.

8:13. And Jesus said to the centurion: Go, and

as thou hast believed, so be it done to thee. And the servant was healed at the same hour.

8:14. And when Jesus was come into Peter's house, he saw his wife's mother lying, and sick of a fever;

8:15. And he touched her hand, and the fever left her, and she arose and ministered to them.

8:16. And when evening was come, they brought to him many that were possessed with devils: and he cast out the spirits with his word: and all that were sick he healed:

8:17. That it might be fulfilled, which was spoken by the prophet Isaias, saying: He took our infirmities, and bore our diseases.

8:18. And Jesus seeing great multitudes about him, gave orders to pass over the water.

8:19. And a certain scribe came and said to him: Master, I will follow thee whithersoever thou shalt go.

8:20. And Jesus saith to him: The foxes have holes, and the birds of the air nests; but the Son of man hath not where to lay his head.

8:21. And another of his disciples said to him: Lord, suffer me first to go and bury my father.

8:22. But Jesus said to him: Follow me, and let the dead bury their dead.

8:23. And when he entered into the boat, his disciples followed him:

8:24. And behold a great tempest arose in the sea, so that the boat was covered with waves, but he was asleep.

8:25. And they came to him, and awaked him, saying: Lord, save us, we perish.

8:26. And Jesus saith to them: Why are you fearful, O ye of little faith? Then rising up, he commanded the winds, and the sea, and there came a great calm.

8:27. But the men wondered, saying: What manner of man is this, for the winds and the sea obey him?

8:28. And when he was come on the other side of the water, into the country of the Gerasens, there met him two that were possessed with devils, coming out of the sepulchres, exceeding fierce, so that none could pass by that way.

8:29. And behold they cried out, saying: What have we to do with thee, Jesus Son of God? art thou come hither to torment us before the time?

8:30. And there was, not far from them, a herd of many swine feeding.

8:31. And the devils besought him, saying: If thou cast us out hence, send us into the herd of swine.

8:32. And he said to them: Go. But they going out went into the swine, and behold the whole herd ran violently down a steep place into the sea: and they perished in the waters.

8:33. And they that kept them fled: and coming into the city, told every thing, and concerning them that had been possessed by the devils.

8:34. And behold the whole city went out to meet Jesus, and when they saw him, they besought him that he would depart from their coast.

Chapter 9

Christ heals one sick of palsy: calls Matthew: cures the issue of blood: raises to life the daughter of Jairus: gives sight to two blind men: and heals a dumb man possessed by the devil.

9:1. And entering into a boat, he passed over the water and came into his own city.

9:2. And behold they brought to him one sick of the palsy lying in a bed. And Jesus, seeing their faith, said to the man sick of the palsy: Be of good heart, son, thy sins are forgiven thee.

9:3. And behold some of the scribes said within themselves: He blasphemeth.

9:4. And Jesus seeing their thoughts, said: Why do you think evil in your hearts?

9:5. Whether is easier, to say, Thy sins are forgiven thee: or to say, Arise, and walk?

9:6. But that you may know that the Son of man hath power on earth to forgive sins, (then said he to the man sick of the palsy,) Arise, take up thy bed, and go into thy house.

9:7. And he arose, and went into his house.

9:8. And the multitude seeing it, feared, and glorified God that gave such power to men.

9:9. And when Jesus passed on from thence, he saw a man sitting in the custom house, named Matthew; and he saith to him: Follow me. And he arose up and followed him.

9:10. And it came to pass as he was sitting at meat in the house, behold many publicans and sinners came, and sat down with Jesus and his disciples.

9:11. And the Pharisees seeing it, said to his disciples: Why doth your master eat with publicans and sinners?

9:12. But Jesus hearing it, said: They that are in health need not a physician, but they that are ill.

9:13. Go then and learn what this meaneth, I will have mercy and not sacrifice. For I am not come to call the just, but sinners.

9:14. Then came to him the disciples of John, saying: Why do we and the Pharisees, fast often, but thy disciples do not fast?

9:15. And Jesus said to them: Can the children of the bridegroom mourn, as long as the bridegroom is with them? But the days will come, when the bridegroom shall be taken away from them, and then they shall fast.

Can the children of the bridegroom... This, by a Hebraism, signifies the friends or companions of the bridegroom.

9:16. And nobody putteth a piece of raw cloth unto an old garment. For it taketh away the fulness thereof from the garment, and there is made a greater rent.

9:17. Neither do they put new wine into old bottles. Otherwise the bottles break, and the wine runneth out, and the bottles perish. But new wine they put into new bottles: and both are preserved.

9:18. As he was speaking these things unto them, behold a certain ruler came up, and adored him, saying: Lord, my daughter is even now dead; but come, lay thy hand upon her, and she shall live.

9:19. And Jesus rising up followed him, with his disciples.

9:20. And behold a woman who was troubled with an issue of blood twelve years, came behind him, and touched the hem of his garment.

9:21. For she said within herself: If I shall touch only his garment, I shall be healed.

9:22. But Jesus turning and seeing her, said: Be of good heart, daughter, thy faith hath made thee whole. And the woman was made whole from that hour.

9:23. And when Jesus was come into the house of the ruler, and saw the minstrels and the multitude making a rout,

9:24. He said: Give place, for the girl is not dead, but sleepeth. And they laughed him to scorn.

9:25. And when the multitude was put forth, he went in, and took her by the hand. And the maid arose.

9:26. And the fame hereof went abroad into all that country.

9:27. And as Jesus passed from thence, there followed him two blind men crying out and saying, Have mercy on us, O Son of David.

9:28. And when he was come to the house, the blind men came to him. And Jesus saith to them, Do you believe, that I can do this unto you? They say to him, Yea, Lord.

9:29. Then he touched their eyes, saying, According to your faith, be it done unto you.

9:30. And their eyes were opened, and Jesus strictly charged them, saying, See that no man know this.

9:31. But they going out, spread his fame abroad in all that country.

9:32. And when they were gone out, behold they brought him a dumb man, possessed with a devil.

9:33. And after the devil was cast out, the dumb man spoke, and the multitudes wondered, saying, Never was the like seen in Israel.

9:34. But the Pharisees said, By the prince of devils he casteth out devils.

9:35. And Jesus went about all the cities and towns, teaching in their synagogues, and preaching the gospel of the kingdom, and healing every disease, and every infirmity.

9:36. And seeing the multitudes, he had compassion on them: because they were distressed, and lying like sheep that have no shepherd.

9:37. Then he saith to his disciples, The harvest indeed is great, but the labourers are few.

9:38. Pray ye therefore the Lord of the harvest, that he send forth labourers into his harvest.

Chapter 10

Christ sends out his twelve apostles, with the power of miracles. The lessons he gives them.

10:1. And having called his twelve disciples together, he gave them power over unclean spirits, to cast them out, and to heal all manner of diseases, and all manner of infirmities.

10:2. And the names of the twelve Apostles are these: The first, Simon who is called Peter, and Andrew his brother,

10:3. James the son of Zebedee, and John his brother, Philip and Bartholomew, Thomas and Matthew the publican, and James the son of Alpheus, and Thaddeus,

10:4. Simon the Cananean, and Judas Iscariot, who also betrayed him.

10:5. These twelve Jesus sent: commanding them, saying: Go ye not into the way of the Gentiles, and into the city of the Samaritans enter ye not.

10:6. But go ye rather to the lost sheep of the house of Israel.

10:7. And going, preach, saying: The kingdom of heaven is at hand.

10:8. Heal the sick, raise the dead, cleanse the

lepers, cast out devils: freely have you received, freely give.

10:9. Do not possess gold, nor silver, nor money in your purses:

10:10. Nor scrip for your journey, nor two coats, nor shoes, nor a staff; for the workman is worthy of his meat.

10:11. And into whatsoever city or town you shall enter, inquire who in it is worthy, and there abide till you go thence.

10:12. And when you come into the house, salute it, saying: Peace be to this house.

10:13. And if that house be worthy, your peace shall come upon it; but if it be not worthy, your peace shall return to you.

10:14. And whosoever shall not receive you, nor hear your words: going forth out of that house or city shake off the dust from your feet.

10:15. Amen I say to you, it shall be more tolerable for the land of Sodom and Gomorrha in the day of judgment, than for that city.

10:16. Behold I send you as sheep in the midst of wolves. Be ye therefore wise as serpents and simple as doves.

Simple... That is, harmless, plain, sincere, and without guile.

10:17. But beware of men. For they will deliver you up in councils, and they will scourge you in their synagogues.

10:18. And you shall be brought before governors, and before kings for my sake, for a testimony to them and to the Gentiles:

10:19. But when they shall deliver you up, take no thought how or what to speak: for it shall be given you in that hour what to speak:

10:20. For it is not you that speak, but the spirit of your Father that speaketh in you.

10:21. The brother also shall deliver up the brother to death, and the father the son; and the children shall rise up against their parents, and shall put them to death.

10:22. And you shall be hated by all men for my name's sake: but he that shall persevere unto the end, he shall be saved.

10:23. And when they shall persecute you in this city, flee into another. Amen I say to you, you shall not finish all the cities of Israel, till the Son of man come.

10:24. The disciple is not above the master, nor the servant above his lord.

10:25. It is enough for the disciple that he be as his master, and the servant as his lord. If they have called the good man of the house Beelzebub, how much more them of his household?

10:26. Therefore fear them not. For nothing is covered that shall not be revealed: nor hid, that shall not be known.

10:27. That which I tell you in the dark, speak ye in the light: and that which you hear in the ear, preach ye upon the housetops.

10:28. And fear ye not them that kill the body, and are not able to kill the soul: but rather fear him that can destroy both soul and body in hell.

10:29. Are not two sparrows sold for a farthing? and not one of them shall fall on the ground without your Father.

10:30. But the very hairs of your head are all numbered.

10:31. Fear not therefore: better are you than many sparrows.

10:32. Every one therefore that shall confess me before men, I will also confess him before my Father who is in heaven.

10:33. But he that shall deny me before men, I will also deny him before my Father who is in heaven.

10:34. Do not think that I came to send peace upon earth: I came not to send peace, but the sword.

10:35. For I came to set a man at variance against his father, and the daughter against her mother, and the daughter in law against her mother in law.

I came to set a man at variance, etc... Not that this was the end or design of the coming of our Saviour; but that his coming and his doctrine would have this effect, by reason of the obstinate resistance that many would make, and of their persecuting all such as should adhere to him.

10:36. And a man's enemies shall be they of his own household.

10:37. He that loveth father or mother more than me, is not worthy of me; and he that loveth son or daughter more than me, is not worthy of me.

10:38. And he that taketh not up his cross, and followeth me, is not worthy of me.

10:39. He that findeth his life, shall lose it: and he that shall lose his life for me, shall find it.

10:40. He that receiveth you, receiveth me: and he that receiveth me, receiveth him that sent me.

10:41. He that receiveth a prophet in the name of a prophet, shall receive the reward of a prophet: and he that receiveth a just man in the name of a just man, shall receive the reward of a just man.

10:42. And whosoever shall give to drink to one of these little ones a cup of cold water only in the name of a disciple, amen I say to you he shall not lose his reward.

Chapter 11

John sends his disciples to Christ, who upbraids the Jews for their incredulity, and calls to him such as are sensible of their burdens.

11:1. And it came to pass, when Jesus had made an end of commanding his twelve disciples, he passed from thence, to teach and to preach in their cities.

11:2. Now when John had heard in prison the works of Christ: sending two of his disciples he said to him:

11:3. Art thou he that art to come, or look we for another?

11:4. And Jesus making answer said to them: Go and relate to John what you have heard and seen.

11:5. The blind see, the lame walk, the lepers are cleansed, the deaf hear, the dead rise again, the poor have the gospel preached to them.

11:6. And blessed is he that shall not be scandalized in me.

Scandalized in me... That is, who shall not take occasion of scandal or offence from my humility, and the disgraceful death of the cross which I shall endure.

11:7. And when they went their way, Jesus began to say to the multitudes concerning John: What went you out into the desert to see? a reed shaken with the wind?

11:8. But what went you out to see? a man clothed in soft garments? Behold they that are clothed in soft garments, are in the houses of kings.

11:9. But what went you out to see? A prophet? Yea I tell you, and more than a prophet.

11:10. For this is he of whom it is written: Behold I send my angel before my face, who shall prepare thy way before thee.

11:11. Amen I say to you, there hath not risen among them that are born of women a greater than John the Baptist: yet he that is the lesser in the kingdom of heaven is greater than he.

11:12. And from the days of John the Baptist until now, the kingdom of heaven suffereth violence, and the violent bear it away.

Suffereth violence, etc... It is not to be obtained but by main force, by using violence upon ourselves, by mortification and penance, and resisting our perverse inclinations.

11:13. For all the prophets and the law prophesied until John:

11:14. And if you will receive it, he is Elias that is to come.

He is Elias, etc... Not in person, but in spirit. St. Luke 1. 17.

11:15. He that hath ears to hear, let him hear.

11:16. But whereunto shall I esteem this generation to be like? It is like to children sitting in the market place.

11:17. Who crying to their companions say: We have piped to you, and you have not danced: we have lamented, and you have not mourned.

11:18. For John came neither eating nor drinking; and they say: He hath a devil.

11:19. The Son of man came eating and drinking, and they say: Behold a man that is a glutton and a wine drinker, a friend of publicans and sinners. And wisdom is justified by her children.

11:20. Then began he to upbraid the cities wherein were done the most of his miracles, for that they had not done penance.

11:21. Woe thee, Corozain, woe to thee, Bethsaida: for if in Tyre and Sidon had been wrought the miracles that have been wrought in you, they had long ago done penance in sackcloth and ashes.

11:22. But I say unto you, it shall be more tolerable for Tyre and Sidon in the day of judgment, than for you.

11:23. And thou Capharnaum, shalt thou be exalted up to heaven? thou shalt go down even unto hell. For if in Sodom had been wrought the miracles that have been wrought in thee, perhaps it had remained unto this day.

11:24. But I say unto you, that it shall be more tolerable for the land of Sodom in the day of judgment than for thee.

11:25. At that time Jesus answered and said: I confess to thee, O Father, Lord of Heaven and earth, because thou hast hid these things from the wise and prudent, and hast revealed them to little ones.

11:26. Yea, Father: for so hath it seemed good in thy sight.

11:27. All things are delivered to me by my Father. And no one knoweth the Son but the Father: neither doth any one know the Father, but the Son, and he to whom it shall please the Son to reveal him.

11:28. Come to me all you that labor and are burdened, and I will refresh you.

11:29. Take up my yoke upon you, and learn of me, because I am meek, and humble of heart: And you shall find rest to your souls.

11:30. For my yoke is sweet and my burden

light.

Chapter 12

Christ reproves the blindness of the Pharisees, and confutes their attributing his miracles to Satan.

12:1. At that time Jesus went through the corn on the sabbath: and his disciples being hungry, began to pluck the ears, and to eat.

12:2. And the Pharisees seeing them, said to him: Behold thy disciples do that which is not lawful to do on the sabbath days.

12:3. But he said to them: Have you not read what David did when he was hungry, and they that were with him:

12:4. How he entered into the house of God, and did eat the loaves of proposition, which it was not lawful for him to eat, nor for them that were with him, but for the priests only?

The loaves of proposition... So were called the twelve loaves which were placed before the sanctuary in the temple of God.

12:5. Or have ye not read in the law, that on the sabbath days the priests in the temple break the sabbath, and are without blame?

12:6. But I tell you that there is here a greater than the temple.

12:7. And if you knew what this meaneth: I will have mercy, and not sacrifice: you would never have condemned the innocent.

12:8. For the Son of man is Lord even of the sabbath.

12:9. And when he had passed from thence, he came into their synagogues.

12:10. And behold there was a man who had a withered hand, and they asked him, saying: Is it lawful to heal on the sabbath days? that they might accuse him.

12:11. But he said to them: What man shall there be among you, that hath one sheep: and if the same fall into a pit on the sabbath day, will he not take hold on it and lift it up?

12:12. How much better is a man than a sheep? Therefore it is lawful to do a good deed on the sabbath days.

12:13. Then he saith to the man: Stretch forth thy hand; and he stretched it forth, and it was restored to health even as the other.

12:14. And the Pharisees going out made a consultation against him, how they might destroy him.

12:15. But Jesus knowing it, retired from thence: and many followed him, and he healed them all.

12:16. And he charged them that they should not make him known.

12:17. That it might be fulfilled which was spoken by Isaias the prophet, saying:

12:18. Behold my servant whom I have chosen, my beloved in whom my soul hath been well pleased. I will put my spirit upon him, and he shall shew judgment to the Gentiles.

12:19. He shall not contend, nor cry out, neither shall any man hear his voice in the streets.

12:20. The bruised reed he shall not break: and smoking flax he shall not extinguish: till he send forth judgment unto victory.

12:21. And in his name the Gentiles shall hope.

12:22. Then was offered to him one possessed with a devil, blind and dumb: and he healed him, so that he spoke and saw.

12:23. And all the multitudes were amazed, and said: Is not this the son of David?

12:24. But the Pharisees hearing it, said: This man casteth not out devils but by Beelzebub the prince of the devils.

12:25. And Jesus knowing their thoughts, said to them: Every kingdom divided against itself shall be made desolate: and every city or house divided against itself shall not stand.

12:26. And if Satan cast out Satan, he is divided against himself: how then shall his kingdom stand?

12:27. And if I by Beelzebub cast out devils, by whom do your children cast them out? Therefore they shall be your judges.

12:28. But if I by the Spirit of God cast out devils, then is the kingdom of God come upon you.

12:29. Or how can any one enter into the house of the strong, and rifle his goods, unless he first bind the strong? and then he will rifle his house.

12:30. He that is not with me, is against me: and he that gathereth not with me, scattereth.

12:31. Therefore I say to you: Every sin and blasphemy shall be forgiven men, but the blasphemy of the Spirit shall not be forgiven.

The blasphemy of the Spirit... The sin here spoken of is that blasphemy, by which the Pharisees attributed the miracles of Christ, wrought by the Spirit of God, to Beelzebub the prince of devils. Now this kind of sin is usually accompanied with so much obstinacy, and such wilful opposing the Spirit of God, and the known truth, that men who are guilty of it, are seldom or never converted: and therefore are never forgiven, because they will not repent. Otherwise there is no sin, which God cannot or will not forgive to such as sincerely repent, and have recourse to the keys of the church.

12:32. And whosoever shall speak a word against the Son of man, it shall be forgiven him: but he that shall speak against the Holy Ghost, it shall not be forgiven him neither in this world, nor in the world to come.

Nor in the world to come... From these words St. Augustine (De Civ. Dei, lib. 21, c. 13) and St. Gregory (Dialog., 4, c. 39) gather, that some sins may be remitted in the world to come; and, consequently, that there is a purgatory or a middle place.

12:33. Either make the tree good and its fruit good: or make the tree evil, and its fruit evil. For by the fruit the tree is known.

12:34. O generation of vipers, how can you speak good things, whereas you are evil? for out of the abundance of the heart the mouth speaketh.

12:35. A good man out of a good treasure bringeth forth good things: and an evil man out of an evil treasure bringeth forth evil things.

12:36. But I say unto you, that every idle word that men shall speak, they shall render an account for it in the day of judgment.

Every idle word... This shews there must be a place of temporal punishment hereafter where these slighter faults shall be punished.

12:37. For by thy words thou shalt be justified, and by thy words thou shalt be condemned.

12:38. Then some of the scribes and Pharisees answered him, saying: Master, we would see a sign from thee.

A sign... That is, a miracle from heaven. St. Luke 11. 16.

12:39. Who answering said to them: An evil and adulterous generation seeketh a sign: and a sign shall not be given it, but the sign of Jonas the prophet.

12:40. For as Jonas was in the whale's belly three days and three nights: so shall the Son of man be in the heart of the earth three days and three nights.

Three days, etc... Not complete days and nights; but part of three days, and three nights taken according to the way that the Hebrews counted their days and nights, viz., from evening to evening.

12:41. The men of Ninive shall rise in judgment with this generation, and shall condemn it: because they did penance at the preaching of Jonas. And behold a greater than Jonas here.

12:42. The queen of the south shall rise in judgment with this generation, and shall condemn it: because she came from the ends of the earth to hear the wisdom of Solomon, and behold a greater than Solomon here.

12:43. And when an unclean spirit is gone out of a man he walketh through dry places seeking rest, and findeth none.

12:44. Then he saith: I will return into my house from whence I came out. And coming he findeth it empty, swept, and garnished.

12:45. Then he goeth, and taketh with him seven other spirits more wicked than himself, and they enter in and dwell there: and the last state of that man is made worse than the first. So shall it be also to this wicked generation.

12:46. As he was yet speaking to the multitudes, behold his mother and his brethren stood without, seeking to speak to him.

12:47. And one said unto him: Behold thy mother and thy brethren stand without, seeking thee.

12:48. But he answering him that told him, said: Who is my mother, and who are my brethren?

Who is my mother?... This was not spoken by way of slighting his mother, but to shew that we are never to suffer ourselves to be taken from the service of God, by any inordinate affection to our earthly parents: and that which our Lord chiefly regarded in his mother, was her doing the will of his Father in heaven. It may also further allude to the reprobation of the Jews, his carnal kindred, and the election of the Gentiles.

12:49. And stretching forth his hand towards his disciples, he said: Behold my mother and my brethren.

12:50. For whosoever shall do the will of my Father, that is in heaven, he is my brother, and sister, and mother.

Chapter 13

The parables of the sower and the cockle: of the mustard seed, etc.

13:1. The same day Jesus going out of the house, sat by the sea side.

13:2. And great multitudes were gathered together unto him, so that he went up into a boat and sat: and all the multitude stood on the shore.

13:3. And he spoke to them many things in parables, saying: Behold the sower went forth to sow.

13:4. And whilst he soweth some fell by the way side, and the birds of the air came and ate them up.

13:5. And other some fell upon stony ground, where they had not much earth: and they sprung up immediately, because they had no deepness of earth.

13:6. And when the sun was up they were scorched: and because they had not root, they withered away.

13:7. And others fell among thorns: and the thorns grew up and choked them.

13:8. And others fell upon good ground: and they brought forth fruit, some an hundred fold, some sixty fold, and some thirty fold.

13:9. He that hath ears to hear, let him hear.

13:10. And his disciples came and said to him: Why speakest thou to them in parables?

13:11. Who answered and said to them: Because to you it is given to know the mysteries of the kingdom of heaven: but to them it is not given.

13:12. For he that hath, to him shall be given, and he shall abound: but he that hath not, from him shall be taken away that also which he hath.

13:13. Therefore do I speak to them in parables: because seeing they see not, and hearing they hear not, neither do they understand.

13:14. And the prophecy of Isaias is fulfilled in them, who saith: By hearing you shall hear, and shall not understand: and seeing you shall see, and shall not perceive.

13:15. For the heart of this people is grown gross, and with their ears they have been dull of hearing, and their eyes they have shut: lest at any time they should see with their eyes, and hear with their ears, and understand with their heart, and be converted, and I should heal them.

13:16. But blessed are your eyes, because they see, and your ears, because they hear.

13:17. For, amen, I say to you, many prophets and just men have desired to see the things that you see, and have not seen them: and to hear the things that you hear and have not heard them.

13:18. Hear you therefore the parable of the sower.

13:19. When any one heareth the word of the kingdom, and understandeth it not, there cometh the wicked one, and catcheth away that which was sown in his heart: this is he that received the seed by the way side.

13:20. And he that received the seed upon stony ground, is he that heareth the word, and immediately receiveth it with joy.

13:21. Yet hath he not root in himself, but is only for a time: and when there ariseth tribulation and persecution because of the word, he is presently scandalized.

13:22. And he that received the seed among thorns, is he that heareth the word, and the care of this world and the deceitfulness of riches choketh up the word, and he becometh fruitless.

13:23. But he that received the seed upon good ground, is he that heareth the word, and understandeth, and beareth fruit, and yieldeth the one an hundredfold, and another sixty, and another thirty.

13:24. Another parable he proposed to them, saying: The kingdom of heaven is likened to a man that sowed good seed in his field.

13:25. But while men were asleep, his enemy came and oversowed cockle among the wheat and went his way.

13:26. And when the blade was sprung up, and had brought forth fruit, then appeared also the cockle.

13:27. And the servants of the good man of the house coming said to him. Sir, didst thou not sow good seed in thy field? Whence then hath it cockle?

13:28. And he said to them: An enemy hath done this. And the servants said to him: Wilt thou that we go and gather it up?

13:29. And he said: No, lest perhaps gathering up the cockle, you root up the wheat also together with it.

13:30. Suffer both to grow until the harvest, and in the time of the harvest I will say to the reapers: Gather up first the cockle, and bind it into bundles to burn, but the wheat gather ye into my barn.

13:31. Another parable he proposed unto them, saying: The kingdom of heaven is like to a grain of mustard seed, which a man took and sowed in his field.

13:32. Which is the least indeed of all seeds; but when it is grown up, it is greater than all herbs, and becometh a tree, so that the birds of the air come, and dwell in the branches thereof.

13:33. Another parable he spoke to them: The kingdom of heaven is like to leaven, which a woman took and hid in three measures of meal, until the whole was leavened.

13:34. All these things Jesus spoke in parables to the multitudes: and without parables he did not speak to them.

13:35. That it might be fulfilled which was spoken by the prophet, saying: I will open my mouth in parables, I will utter things hidden from the foundation of the world.

13:36. Then having sent away the multitudes, he came into the house, and his disciples came to him, saying: Expound to us the parable of the cockle of the field.

13:37. Who made answer and said to them: He that soweth the good seed is the Son of man.

13:38. And the field is the world. And the good seed are the children of the kingdom. And the cockle are the children of the wicked one.

13:39. And the enemy that sowed them, is the devil. But the harvest is the end of the world. And the reapers are the angels.

13:40. Even as cockle therefore is gathered up, and burnt with fire: so shall it be at the end of the world.

13:41. The Son of man shall send his angels, and

they shall gather out of his kingdom all scandals, and them that work iniquity.

13:42. And shall cast them into the furnace of fire: there shall be weeping and gnashing of teeth.

13:43. Then shall the just shine as the sun, in the kingdom of their Father. He that hath ears to hear, let him hear.

13:44. The kingdom of heaven is like unto a treasure hidden in a field. Which a man having found, hid it, and for joy thereof goeth, and selleth all that he hath, and buyeth that field.

13:45. Again the kingdom of heaven is like to a merchant seeking good pearls.

13:46. Who when he had found one pearl of great price, went his way, and sold all that he had, and bought it.

13:47. Again the kingdom of heaven is like to a net cast into the sea, and gathering together of all kinds of fishes.

13:48. Which, when it was filled, they drew out, and sitting by the shore, they chose out the good into vessels, but the bad they cast forth.

13:49. So shall it be at the end of the world. The angels shall go out, and shall separate the wicked from among the just.

13:50. And shall cast them into the furnace of

fire: there shall be weeping and gnashing of teeth.

13:51. Have ye understood all these things? They say to him: Yes.

13:52. He said unto them: Therefore every scribe instructed in the kingdom of heaven, is like to a man that is a householder, who bringeth forth out of his treasure new things and old.

13:53. And it came to pass: when Jesus had finished these parables, he passed from thence.

13:54. And coming into his own country, he taught them in their synagogues, so that they wondered and said: How came this man by this wisdom and miracles?

13:55. Is not this the carpenter's son? Is not his mother called Mary, and his brethren James, and Joseph, and Simon, and Jude:

His brethren... These were the children of Mary the wife of Cleophas, sister to our Blessed Lady, (St. Matt. 27. 56; St. John 19. 25,) and therefore, according to the usual style of the Scripture, they were called brethren, that is, near relations to our Saviour.

13:56. And his sisters, are they not all with us? Whence therefore hath he all these things?

13:57. And they were scandalized in his regard. But Jesus said to them: A prophet is not without honour, save in his own country, and in his own house.

13:58. And he wrought not many miracles there, because of their unbelief.

Chapter 14

Herod puts John to death. Christ feeds five thousand in the desert. He walks upon the sea, and heals all the diseased with the touch of his garment.

14:1. At that time Herod the Tetrarch heard the fame of Jesus.

Tetrarch... This word, derived from the Greek, signifies one that rules over the fourth part of a kingdom: as Herod then ruled over Galilee, which was but the fourth part of the kingdom of his father.

14:2. And he said to his servants: This is John the Baptist: he is risen from the dead, and therefore mighty works shew forth themselves in him.

14:3. For Herod had apprehended John and bound him, and put him into prison, because of Herodias, his brother's wife.

14:4. For John said to him: It is not lawful for thee to have her.

14:5. And having a mind to put him to death, he feared the people: because they esteemed him as a prophet.

14:6. But on Herod's birthday, the daughter of Herodias danced before them: and pleased Herod.

14:7. Whereupon he promised with an oath, to give her whatsoever she would ask of him.

14:8. But she being instructed before by her mother, said: Give me here in a dish the head of John the Baptist.

14:9. And the king was struck sad: yet because of his oath, and for them that sat with him at table, he commanded it to be given.

14:10. And he sent, and beheaded John in the prison.

14:11. And his head was brought in a dish: and it was given to the damsel, and she brought it to her mother.

14:12. And his disciples came and took the body, and buried it, and came and told Jesus.

14:13. Which when Jesus had heard, he retired from thence by a boat, into a desert place apart, and the multitudes having heard of it, followed him on foot out of the cities.

14:14. And he coming forth saw a great multitude, and had compassion on them, and healed their sick.

14:15. And when it was evening, his disciples came to him, saying: This is a desert place, and the hour is now passed: send away the multitudes, that going into the towns, they may buy themselves victuals.

14:16. But Jesus said to them, They have no need to go: give you them to eat.

14:17. They answered him: We have not here, but five loaves, and two fishes.

14:18. Who said to them: Bring them hither to me.

14:19. And when he had commanded the multitude to sit down upon the grass, he took the five loaves and the two fishes, and looking up to heaven, he blessed, and brake, and gave the loaves to his disciples, and the disciples to the multitudes.

14:20. And they did all eat, and were filled. And they took up what remained, twelve full baskets of fragments.

14:21. And the number of them that did eat, was five thousand men, besides women and children.

14:22. And forthwith Jesus obliged his disciples to go up into the boat, and to go before him over the water, till he dismissed the people.

14:23. And having dismissed the multitude, he went into a mountain alone to pray. And when it was evening, he was there alone.

14:24. But the boat in the midst of the sea was tossed with the waves: for the wind was contrary.

14:25. And in the fourth watch of the night, he came to them walking upon the sea.

14:26. And they seeing him walking upon the sea, were troubled, saying: It is an apparition. And they cried out for fear.

14:27. And immediately Jesus spoke to them, saying: Be of good heart: it is I, fear ye not.

14:28. And Peter making answer, said: Lord, if it be thou, bid me come to thee upon the waters.

14:29. And he said: Come. And Peter going down out of the boat walked upon the water to come to Jesus.

14:30. But seeing the wind strong, he was afraid: and when he began to sink, he cried out, saying: Lord, save me.

14:31. And immediately Jesus stretching forth his hand took hold of him, and said to him: O thou of little faith, why didst thou doubt?

14:32. And when they were come up into the boat, the wind ceased.

14:33. And they that were in the boat came and adored him, saying: Indeed thou art the Son of God.

14:34. And having passed the water, they came into the country of Genesar.

14:35. And when the men of that place had knowledge of him, they sent into all that country, and brought to him all that were diseased.

14:36. And they besought him that they might touch but the hem of his garment. And as many as touched, were made whole.

Chapter 15

Christ reproves the Scribes. He cures the daughter of the woman of Canaan: and many others: and feeds four thousand with seven loaves.

15:1. Then came to him from Jerusalem scribes and Pharisees, saying:

15:2. Why do thy disciples transgress the tradition of the ancients? For they wash not their hands when they eat bread.

15:3. But he answering, said to them: Why do you also transgress the commandment of God for your tradition? For God said:

15:4. Honour thy father and mother: And: He that shall curse father or mother, let him die the death.

15:5. But you say: Whosoever shall say to father or mother, The gift whatsoever proceedeth from me, shall profit thee.

The gift, etc... That is, the offering that I shall

make to God, shall be instead of that which should be expended for thy profit. This tradition of the Pharisees was calculated to enrich themselves; by exempting children from giving any further assistance to their parents, if they once offered to the temple and the priests, that which should have been the support of their parents. But this was a violation of the law of God, and of nature, which our Saviour here condemns.

15:6. And he shall not honour his father or his mother: and you have made void the commandment of God for your tradition.

15:7. Hypocrites, well hath Isaias prophesied of you, saying:

15:8. This people honoureth me with their lips: but their heart is far from me.

15:9. And in vain do they worship me, teaching doctrines and commandments of men.

Commandments of men... The doctrines and commandments here reprehended are such as are either contrary to the law of God, (as that of neglecting parents, under pretence of giving to God,) or at least are frivolous, unprofitable, and no ways conducing to true piety, as that of often washing hands, etc., without regard to the purity of the heart. But as to the rules and ordinances of the holy church, touching fasts, festivals, etc., these are no ways repugnant to, but highly agreeable to God's holy word, and all Christian piety: neither are they to be counted among the doctrines and commandments of men; because they proceed not from mere human authority; but from that which Christ has established in his church; whose pastors he has commanded us to hear and obey, even as himself. St. Luke 10. 16; St. Matt. 18. 17.

15:10. And having called together the multitudes unto him, he said to them: Hear ye and understand.

15:11. Not that which goeth into the mouth defileth a man: but what cometh out of the mouth, this defileth a man.

Not that which goeth into, etc... No uncleanness in meat, nor any dirt contracted by eating it with unwashed hands, can defile the soul: but sin alone; or a disobedience of the heart to the ordinance and will of God. And thus when Adam took the forbidden fruit, it was not the apple, which entered into the mouth, but the disobedience to the law of God which defiled him. The same is to be said if a Jew, in the time of the old law, had eaten swine's flesh; or a Christian convert, in the days of the apostles, contrary to their ordinance, had eaten blood; or if any of the faithful at present should transgress the ordinance of God's church, by breaking the fasts: for in all these cases the soul would be defiled; not indeed by that which goeth into the mouth; but by the disobedience of the heart, in wilfully transgressing the ordinance of God, or of those who have their authority from him.

15:12. Then came his disciples, and said to him: Dost thou know that the Pharisees, when they heard this word, were scandalized?

15:13. But he answering, said: Every plant which my heavenly Father hath not planted, shall be rooted up.

15:14. Let them alone: they are blind, and leaders of the blind. And if the blind lead the blind, both fall into the pit.

15:15. And Peter answering, said to him: Expound to us this parable.

15:16. But he said: Are you also yet without understanding?

15:17. Do you not understand, that whatsoever entereth into the mouth, goeth into the belly, and is cast out into the privy?

15:18. But the things which proceed out of the mouth, come forth from the heart, and those things defile a man.

15:19. For from the heart come forth evil thoughts, murders, adulteries, fornications, thefts, false testimonies, blasphemies.

15:20. These are the things that defile a man. But to eat with unwashed hands doth not defile a man.

15:21. And Jesus went from thence, and retired into the coast of Tyre and Sidon.

15:22. And behold a woman of Canaan who

came out of those coasts, crying out, said to him: Have mercy on me, O Lord, thou son of David: my daughter is grievously troubled by a devil.

15:23. Who answered her not a word. And his disciples came and besought him, saying: Send her away, for she crieth after us:

15:24. And he answering, said: I was not sent but to the sheep, that are lost of the house of Israel.

15:25. But she came and adored him, saying: Lord, help me.

15:26. Who answering, said: It is not good to take the bread of the children, and to cast it to the dogs.

15:27. But she said: Yea, Lord; for the whelps also eat of the crumbs that fall from the table of their masters.

15:28. Then Jesus answering, said to her: O woman, great is thy faith: be it done to thee as thou wilt: and her daughter was cured from that hour.

15:29. And when Jesus had passed away from thence, he came nigh the sea of Galilee: and going up into a mountain, he sat there.

15:30. And there came to him great multitudes, having with them the dumb, the blind, the lame, the maimed, and many others: and they cast them down at his feet, and he healed them:

15:31. So that the multitudes marvelled seeing the dumb speak, the lame walk, the blind see: and they glorified the God of Israel.

15:32. And Jesus called together his disciples, and said: I have compassion on the multitudes, because they continue with me now three days, and have not what to eat, and I will not send them away fasting, lest they faint in the way.

15:33. And the disciples say unto him: Whence then should we have so many loaves in the desert, as to fill so great a multitude?

15:34. And Jesus said to them: How many loaves have you? But they said: Seven, and a few little fishes.

15:35. And he commanded the multitude to sit down upon the ground.

15:36. And taking the seven loaves and the fishes, and giving thanks, he brake, and gave to his disciples, and the disciples gave to the people.

15:37. And they did all eat, and had their fill. And they took up seven baskets full, of what remained of the fragments.

15:38. And they that did eat, were four thousand men, beside children and women.

15:39. And having dismissed the multitude, he went up into a boat, and came into the coasts of Magedan.

Chapter 16

Christ refuses to shew the Pharisees a sign from heaven. Peter's confession is rewarded. He is rebuked for opposing Christ's passion. All his followers must deny themselves.

16:1. And there came to him the Pharisees and Sadducees tempting: and they asked him to shew them a sign from heaven.

16:2. But he answered and said to them: When it is evening, you say, It will be fair weather, for the sky is red.

16:3. And in the morning: To day there will be a storm, for the sky is red and lowering. You know then how to discern the face of the sky: and can you not know the signs of the times?

16:4. A wicked and adulterous generation seeketh after a sign: and a sign shall not be given it, but the sign of Jonas the prophet. And he left them, and went away.

16:5. And when his disciples were come over the water, they had forgotten to take bread.

16:6. Who said to them: Take heed and beware of the leaven of the Pharisees and Sadducees.

16:7. But they thought within themselves, saying: Because we have taken no bread.
16:8. And Jesus knowing it, said: Why do you

think within yourselves, O ye of little faith, for that you have no bread?

16:9. Do you not yet understand, neither do you remember the five loaves among five thousand men, and how many baskets you took up?

16:10. Nor the seven loaves, among four thousand men, and how many baskets you took up?

16:11. Why do you not understand that it was not concerning bread I said to you: Beware of the leaven of the Pharisees and Sadducees?

16:12. Then they understood that he said not that they should beware of the leaven of bread, but of the doctrine of the Pharisees and Sadducees.

16:13. And Jesus came into the quarters of Cesarea Philippi: and he asked his disciples, saying: Whom do men say that the Son of man is?

16:14. But they said: Some John the Baptist, and other some Elias, and others Jeremias, or one of the prophets.

16:15. Jesus saith to them: But whom do you say that I am?

16:16. Simon Peter answered and said: Thou art Christ, the Son of the living God.

16:17. And Jesus answering said to him: Blessed art thou, Simon Bar-Jona: because flesh and blood hath not revealed it to thee, but my Father who is in heaven.

16:18. And I say to thee: That thou art Peter; and upon this rock I will build my church, and the gates of hell shall not prevail against it.

Thou art Peter, etc... As St. Peter, by divine revelation, here made a solemn profession of his faith of the divinity of Christ; so in recompense of this faith and profession, our Lord here declares to him the dignity to which he is pleased to raise him: viz., that he to whom he had already given the name of Peter, signifying a rock, St. John 1. 42, should be a rock indeed, of invincible strength, for the support of the building of the church; in which building he should be, next to Christ himself, the chief foundation stone, in quality of chief pastor, ruler, and governor; and should have accordingly all fulness of ecclesiastical power, signified by the keys of the kingdom of heaven.

Upon this rock, etc... The words of Christ to Peter, spoken in the vulgar language of the Jews which our Lord made use of, were the same as if he had said in English, Thou art a Rock, and upon this rock I will build my church. So that, by the plain course of the words, Peter is here declared to be the rock, upon which the church was to be built: Christ himself being both the principal foundation and founder of the same. Where also note, that Christ, by building his house, that is, his church, upon a rock, has thereby secured it against all storms and floods, like the wise builder, St. Matt. 7. 24, 25. The gates of hell, etc... That is, the powers of darkness, and whatever Satan can do, either by himself, or his agents. For as the church is here likened to a house, or fortress, built on a rock; so the adverse powers are likened to a contrary house or fortress, the gates of which, that is, the whole strength, and all the efforts it can make, will never be able to prevail over the city or church of Christ. By this promise we are fully assured, that neither idolatry, heresy, nor any pernicious error whatsoever shall at any time prevail over the church of Christ.

16:19. And I will give to thee the keys of the kingdom of heaven. And whatsoever thou shalt bind upon earth, it shall be bound also in heaven: and whatsoever thou shalt loose on earth, it shall be loosed also in heaven.

Loose on earth... The loosing the bands of temporal punishments due to sins, is called an indulgence; the power of which is here granted.

16:20. Then he commanded his disciples, that they should tell no one that he was Jesus the Christ.

16:21. From that time Jesus began to shew to his disciples, that he must go to Jerusalem, and suffer many things from the ancients and scribes and chief priests, and be put to death, and the third day rise again.

16:22. And Peter taking him, began to rebuke him, saying: Lord, be it far from thee, this shall not be unto thee.

And Peter taking him... That is, taking him aside, out of a tender love, respect and zeal for his Lord and Master's honour, began to expostulate with him, as it were to rebuke him, saying, Lord, far be it from thee to suffer death; but the Lord said to Peter, ver. 23, Go behind me, Satan. These words may signify, Begone from me; but the holy Fathers expound them otherwise, that is, come after me, or follow me; and by these words the Lord would have Peter to follow him in his suffering, and not to oppose the divine will by contradiction; for the word satan means in Hebrew an adversary, or one that opposes.

16:23. Who turning, said to Peter: Go behind me, Satan, thou art a scandal unto me: because thou savourest not the things that are of God, but the things that are of men.

16:24. Then Jesus said to his disciples: If any man will come after me, let him deny himself, and take up his cross, and follow me.

16:25. For he that will save his life, shall lose it: and he that shall lose his life for my sake, shall find it.

16:26. For what doth it profit a man, if he gain the whole world and suffer the loss of his own soul? Or what exchange shall a man give for his soul?

16:27. For the Son of man shall come in the glory of his Father with his angels: and then will he render to every man according to his works.

16:28. Amen I say to you, there are some of them that stand here, that shall not taste death, till they see the Son of man coming in his kingdom.

Chapter 17

The Transfiguration of Christ: He cures the lunatic child: foretells his passion; and pays the didrachma.

17:1. And after six days Jesus taketh unto him Peter and James, and John his brother, and bringeth them up into a high mountain apart:

17:2. And he was transfigured before them. And his face did shine as the sun: and his garments became white as snow.

17:3. And behold there appeared to them Moses and Elias talking with him.

17:4. And Peter answering, said to Jesus: Lord, it is good for us to be here: if thou wilt, let us make here three tabernacles, one for thee, and one for Moses, and one for Elias.

17:5. And as he was yet speaking, behold a bright cloud overshadowed them. And lo a voice out of the cloud, saying: This is my beloved Son, in whom I am well pleased: hear ye him.

17:6. And the disciples hearing fell upon their face, and were very much afraid.

17:7. And Jesus came and touched them: and said to them: Arise, and fear not.

17:8. And they lifting up their eyes, saw no one, but only Jesus.

17:9. And as they came down from the mountain, Jesus charged them, saying: Tell the vision to no man, till the Son of man be risen from the dead.

17:10. And his disciples asked him, saying: Why then do the scribes say that Elias must come first?

17:11. But he answering, said to them: Elias indeed shall come, and restore all things.

17:12. But I say to you, that Elias is already come, and they knew him not, But have done unto him whatsoever they had a mind. So also the Son of man shall suffer from them.

17:13. Then the disciples understood, that he had spoken to them of John the Baptist.

17:14. And when he was come to the multitude, there came to him a man falling down on his knees before him saying: Lord, have pity on my son, for he is a lunatic, and suffereth much: for he falleth often into the fire, and often into the water.

17:15. And I brought him to thy disciples, and they could not cure him.

17:16. Then Jesus answered and said: O unbelieving and perverse generation, how long shall I be with you? How long shall I suffer you? Bring him hither to me.

17:17. And Jesus rebuked him, and the devil went out of him, and the child was cured from that hour.

17:18. Then came the disciples to Jesus secretly, and said: Why could not we cast him out?

17:19. Jesus said to them: Because of your unbelief. For, amen I say to you, if you have faith as a grain of mustard seed, you shall say to this mountain: Remove from hence hither, and it shall remove: and nothing shall be impossible to you.

As a grain of mustard seed... That is, a perfect faith; which in its properties, and its fruits, resembles the grain of mustard seed, in the parable, chap. 13. 31.

17:20. But this kind is not cast out but by prayer and fasting.

17:21. And when they abode together in Galilee, Jesus said to them: The Son of man shall be betrayed into the hands of men:

17:22. And they shall kill him, and the third day he shall rise again. And they were troubled exceedingly.

17:23. And when they were come to Capharnaum, they that received the didrachmas, came to Peter, and said to him: Doth not your master pay the didrachma?

The didrachmas... A didrachma was half a sicle, or half a stater; that is, about 15d. English: which was a tax laid upon every head for the service of the temple.

17:24. He said: Yes. And when he was come into the house, Jesus prevented him, saying: What is thy opinion, Simon? The kings of the earth, of whom do they receive tribute or custom, of their own children, or of strangers?

17:25. And he said: Of strangers. Jesus said to him: Then the children are free.

17:26. But that we may not scandalize them, go to the sea, and cast in a hook: and that fish which shall first come up, take: and when thou hast opened it's mouth, thou shalt find a stater: take that, and give it to them for me and thee.

Chapter 18

Christ teaches humility, to beware of scandal, and to flee the occasions of sin: to denounce to the church incorrigible sinners, and to look upon such as refuse to hear the church as heathens. He promises to his disciples the power of binding and loosing: and that he will be in the midst of their assemblies. No forgiveness for them that will not forgive.

18:1. At that hour the disciples came to Jesus, saying: Who, thinkest thou, is the greater in the kingdom of heaven?

18:2. And Jesus, calling unto him a little child, set him in the midst of them.

18:3. And said: amen I say to you, unless you be converted, and become as little children, you shall not enter into the kingdom of heaven.

18:4. Whosoever therefore shall humble himself as this little child, he is the greater in the kingdom of heaven.

18:5. And he that shall receive one such little child in my name, receiveth me.

18:6. But he that shall scandalize one of these little ones that believe in me, it were better for him that a millstone should be hanged about his neck, and that he should be drowned in the depth of the sea.

Shall scandalize... That is, shall put a stumbling-block in their way, and cause them to fall into sin.

18:7. Woe to the world because of scandals. For it must needs be that scandals come: but nevertheless woe to that man by whom the scandal cometh.

It must needs be, etc... Viz., considering the wickedness and corruption of the world.

18:8. And if thy hand, or thy foot, scandalize thee, cut it off, and cast it from thee. It is better for thee to go into life maimed or lame, than having two hands or two feet, to be cast into everlasting fire.
Scandalize thee... That is, cause thee to offend.

18:9. And if thy eye scandalize thee, pluck it out,

and cast it from thee. It is better for thee having one eye to enter into life, than having two eyes to be cast into hell fire.

18:10. See that you despise not one of these little ones: for I say to you, that their angels in heaven always see the face of my Father who is in heaven.

18:11. For the Son of man is come to save that which was lost.

18:12. What think you? If a man have an hundred sheep, and one of them should go astray: doth he not leave the ninety-nine in the mountains, and goeth to seek that which is gone astray?

18:13. And if it so be that he find it: Amen I say to you, he rejoiceth more for that, than for the ninety-nine that went not astray.

18:14. Even so it is not the will of your Father, who is in heaven, that one of these little ones should perish.

18:15. But if thy brother shall offend against thee, go, and rebuke him between thee and him alone. If he shall hear thee, thou shalt gain thy brother.

18:16. And if he will not hear thee, take with thee one or two more: that in the mouth of two or three witnesses every word may stand.

18:17. And if he will not hear them: tell the church. And if he will not hear the church, let him be to thee as the heathen and publican.

18:18. Amen I say to you, whatsoever you shall bind upon earth, shall be bound also in heaven: and whatsoever you shall loose upon earth, shall be loosed also in heaven.

18:19. Again I say to you, that if two of you shall consent upon earth, concerning anything whatsoever they shall ask, it shall be done to them by my Father who is in heaven.

18:20. For where there are two or three gathered together in my name, there am I in the midst of them.

There am I in the midst of them... This is understood of such assemblies only as are gathered in the name and authority of Christ; and in unity of the church of Christ. St. Cyprian, De Unitate Ecclesiae.

18:21. Then came Peter unto him and said: Lord, how often shall my brother offend against me, and I forgive him? till seven times?

18:22. Jesus saith to him: I say not to thee, till seven times; but till seventy times seven times.

18:23. Therefore is the kingdom of heaven likened to a king, who would take an account of his servants.

18:24. And when he had begun to take the account, one as brought to him, that owed him ten thousand talents.

Talents... A talent was seven hundred and fifty ounces of silver, which at the rate of five shillings to the ounce is a hundred and eighty-seven pounds ten shillings sterling.

18:25. And as he had not wherewith to pay it, his lord commanded that he should be sold, and his wife and children, and all that he had, and payment to be made.

18:26. But that servant falling down, besought him, saying: Have patience with me, and I will pay thee all.

18:27. And the lord of that servant being moved with pity, let him go and forgave him the debt.

18:28. But when that servant was gone out, he found one of his fellow- servants that owed him an hundred pence: and laying hold of him, he throttled him, saying: Pay what thou owest.

Pence... The Roman penny was the eighth part of an ounce, that is, about sevenpence half-penny English.

18:29. And his fellow-servant falling down, besought him, saying: Have patience with me, and I will pay thee all.

18:30. And he would not: but went and cast him into prison, till he paid the debt.

18:31. Now his fellow servants seeing what was done, were very much grieved, and they came, and told their lord all that was done.

18:32. Then his lord called him: and said to him: Thou wicked servant, I forgave thee all the debt, because thou besoughtest me:

18:33. Shouldst not thou then have had compassion also on thy fellow servant, even as I had compassion on thee?

18:34. And his lord being angry, delivered him to the torturers until he paid all the debt.

18:35. So also shall my heavenly Father do to you, if you forgive not every one his brother from your hearts.

Chapter 19

Christ declares matrimony to be indissoluble: he recommends the making one's self an eunuch for the kingdom of heaven; and parting with all things for him. He shews the danger of riches, and the reward of leaving all to follow him.

19:1. And it came to pass when Jesus had ended these words, he departed from Galilee and came into the coasts of Judea, beyond Jordan.

19:2. And great multitudes followed him: and he healed them there.

19:3. And there came to him the Pharisees tempting him, saying: Is it lawful for a man to put away his wife for every cause?

19:4. Who answering, said to them: Have ye not read, that he who made man from the beginning, made them male and female? And he said:

19:5. For this cause shall a man leave father and mother, and shall cleave to his wife, and they two shall be in one flesh.

19:6. Therefore now they are not two, but one flesh. What therefore God hath joined together, let no man put asunder.

19:7. They say to him: Why then did Moses command to give a bill of divorce, and to put away?

19:8. He saith to them: Because Moses by reason of the hardness of your heart permitted you to put away your wives: but from the beginning it was not so.

19:9. And I say to you, that whosoever shall put away his wife, except it be for fornication, and shall marry another, committeth adultery: and he that shall marry her that is put away, committeth adultery.

Except it be, etc... In the case of fornication, that is, of adultery, the wife may be put away: but even then the husband cannot marry another as long as the wife is living.

19:10. His disciples say unto him: If the case of a man with his wife be so, it is not expedient to marry.

19:11. Who said to them: All men take not this word, but they to whom it is given.

All men take not this word... That is, all receive not the gift of living singly and chastely, unless they pray for the grace of God to enable them to live so, and for some it may be necessary to that end to fast as well as pray: and to those it is given from above.

19:12. For there are eunuchs, who were born so from their mothers womb: and there are eunuchs, who were made so by men: and there are eunuchs, who have made themselves eunuchs for the kingdom of heaven. He that can take, let him take it.

There are eunuchs, who have made themselves eunuchs, for the kingdom of heaven... This text is not to be taken in the literal sense; but means, that there are such, who have taken a firm and commendable resolution of leading a single and chaste life, in order to serve God in a more perfect state than those who marry: as St. Paul clearly shews. 1 Cor. 7. 37, 38.

19:13. Then were little children presented to him, that he should impose hands upon them and pray. And the disciples rebuked them.

19:14. But Jesus said to them: Suffer the little children, and forbid them not to come to me: for the kingdom of heaven is for such.

19:15. And when he had imposed hands upon them, he departed from thence.

19:16. And behold one came and said to him: Good master, what good shall I do that I may have life everlasting?

19:17. Who said to him: Why askest thou me concerning good? One is good, God. But if thou wilt enter into life, keep the commandments.

19:18. He said to him: Which? And Jesus said: Thou shalt do no murder, Thou shalt not commit adultery, Thou shalt not steal, Thou shalt not bear false witness.

19:19. Honour thy father and thy mother: and, Thou shalt love thy neighbor as thyself.

19:20. The young man saith to him: All these have I kept from my youth, what is yet wanting to me?

19:21. Jesus saith to him: If thou wilt be perfect, go sell what thou hast, and give to the poor, and thou shalt have treasure in heaven: and come, follow me.

19:22. And when the young man had heard this word, he went away sad: for he had great possessions.

19:23. Then Jesus said to his disciples: Amen, I say to you, that a rich man shall hardly enter into the kingdom of heaven.

19:24. And again I say to you: It is easier for a

camel to pass through the eye of a needle, than for a rich man to enter into the kingdom of heaven.

19:25. And when they had heard this, the disciples wondered much, saying: Who then can be saved?

19:26. And Jesus beholding, said to them: With men this is impossible: but with God all things are possible.

19:27. Then Peter answering, said to him: Behold we have left all things, and have followed thee: what therefore shall we have?

19:28. And Jesus said to them: Amen I say to you, that you who have followed me, in the regeneration, when the Son of man shall sit on the seat of his majesty, you also shall sit on twelve seats judging the twelve tribes of Israel.

19:29. And every one that hath left house, or brethren, or sisters, or father, or mother, or wife, or children, or lands for my name's sake, shall receive an hundredfold, and shall possess life everlasting.

19:30. And many that are first, shall be last: and the last shall be first.

Chapter 20

The parable of the labourers in the vineyard. The ambition of the two sons of Zebedee. Christ gives sight to two blind men.

20:1. The kingdom of heaven is like to an householder, who went out early in the morning to hire labourers into his vineyard.

20:2. And having agreed with the labourers for a penny a day, he sent them into his vineyard.

20:3. And going out about the third hour, he saw others standing in the marketplace idle.

20:4. And he said to them: Go you also into my vineyard, and I will give you what shall be just.

20:5. And they went their way. And again he went out about the sixth and the ninth hour, and did in like manner.

20:6. But about the eleventh hour he went out and found others standing, and he saith to them: Why stand you here all the day idle?

20:7. They say to him: Because no man hath hired us. He saith to them: Go ye also into my vineyard.

20:8. And when evening was come, the lord of the vineyard saith to his steward: Call the labourers and pay them their hire, beginning from the last even to the first.

20:9. When therefore they were come that came about the eleventh hour, they received every man a penny.

20:10. But when the first also came, they thought that they should receive more: And they also received every man a penny.

20:11. And receiving it they murmured against the master of the house,

20:12. Saying: These last have worked but one hour and thou hast made them equal to us, that have borne the burden of the day and the heats.

20:13. But he answering said to one of them: friend, I do thee no wrong: didst thou not agree with me for a penny?

20:14. Take what is thine, and go thy way: I will also give to this last even as to thee.

20:15. Or, is it not lawful for me to do what I will? Is thy eye evil, because I am good?

What I will... Viz., with my own, and in matters that depend on my own bounty.

20:16. So shall the last be first and the first last. For many are called but few chosen.

20:17. And Jesus going up to Jerusalem, took the twelve disciples apart and said to them:

20:18. Behold we go up to Jerusalem, and the Son of man shall be betrayed to the chief priests and the scribes: and they shall condemn him to death.

20:19. And shall deliver him to the Gentiles to be mocked and scourged and crucified: and the third day he shall rise again.

20:20. Then came to him the mother of the sons of Zebedee with her sons, adoring and asking something of him.

20:21. Who said to her: What wilt thou? She saith to him: say that these my two sons may sit, the one on thy right hand, and the other on thy left, in thy kingdom.

20:22. And Jesus answering, said: You know not what you ask. Can you drink the chalice that I shall drink? They say to him: We can.

20:23. He saith to them: My chalice indeed you shall drink; but to sit on my right or left hand is not mine to give to you, but to them for whom it is prepared by my Father.

20:24. And the ten, hearing it, were moved with indignation against the two brethren.

20:25. But Jesus called them to him and said: You know that the princes of the Gentiles lord it over them; and that they that are the greater, exercise power upon them.

20:26. It shall not be so among you: but whosoever is the greater among you, let him be your minister.

20:27. And he that will be first among you shall be your servant.

20:28. Even as the Son of man is not come to be ministered unto, but to minister and to give his life a redemption for many.

20:29. And when they went out from Jericho, a great multitude followed him.

20:30. And behold two blind men sitting by the way side heard that Jesus passed by. And they cried out, saying: O Lord, thou son of David, have mercy on us.

20:31. And the multitude rebuked them that they should hold their peace. But they cried out the more, saying: O Lord, thou son of David, have mercy on us.

20:32. And Jesus stood and called them and said: What will ye that I do to you?

20:33. They say to him: Lord, that our eyes be opened.

20:34. And Jesus having compassion on them, touched their eyes. And immediately they saw and followed him.

Matthew Chapter 21

Christ rides into Jerusalem upon an ass. He casts the buyers and sellers out of the temple, curses the fig tree and puts to silence the priests and scribes.

21:1. And when they drew nigh to Jerusalem and were come to Bethphage, unto mount Olivet, then Jesus sent two disciples,

21:2. Saying to them: Go ye into the village that is over against you: and immediately you shall find an ass tied and a colt with her. Loose them and bring them to me.

21:3. And if any man shall say anything to you, say ye that the Lord hath need of them. And forthwith he will let them go.

21:4. Now all this was done that it might be fulfilled which was spoken by the prophet, saying:

21:5. Tell ye the daughter of Sion: Behold thy king cometh to thee, meek and sitting upon an ass and a colt, the foal of her that is used to the yoke.

21:6. And the disciples going, did as Jesus commanded them.

21:7. And they brought the ass and the colt and laid their garments upon them and made him sit thereon.

21:8. And a very great multitude spread their garments in the way: and others cut boughs from the trees and strewed them in the way.

21:9. And the multitudes that went before and that followed cried, saying: Hosanna to the son of David: Blessed is he that cometh in the name of the Lord: Hosanna in the highest.

21:10. And when he was come into Jerusalem, the whole city was moved, saying: Who is this?

21:11. And the people said: This is Jesus, the prophet from Nazareth of Galilee.

21:12. And Jesus went into the temple of God and cast out all them that sold and bought in the temple and overthrew the tables of the money changers and the chairs of them that sold doves.

21:13. And he saith to them: It is written, My house shall be called the house of prayer; but you have made it a den of thieves.

21:14. And there came to him the blind and the lame in the temple: and he healed them.

21:15. And the chief priests and scribes, seeing the wonderful things that he did and the children crying in the temple and saying: Hosanna to the son of David, were moved with indignation,

21:16. And said to him: Hearest thou what these say? And Jesus said to them: Yea, have you never read: Out of the mouth of infants and of sucklings thou hast perfected praise?

21:17. And leaving them, he went out of the city into Bethania and remained there.

21:18. And in the morning, returning into the city, he was hungry.

21:19. And seeing a certain fig tree by the way side, he came to it and found nothing on it but leaves only. And he saith to it: May no fruit grow on thee henceforward for ever. And immediately the fig tree withered away.

21:20. And the disciples seeing it wondered, saying: How is it presently withered away?

21:21. And Jesus answering, said to them: Amen, I say to you, if you shall have faith and stagger not, not only this of the fig tree shall you do, but also if you shall say to this mountain, Take up and cast thyself into the sea, it shall be done.

21:22. And all things whatsoever you shall ask in prayer believing, you shall receive.

21:23. And when he was come into the temple, there came to him, as he was teaching, the chief priests and ancients of the people, saying: By what authority dost thou these things? And who hath given thee this authority?

21:24. Jesus answering, said to them: I also will ask you one word, which if you shall tell me, I will also tell you by what authority I do these things.

21:25. The baptism of John, whence was it? From heaven or from men? But they thought within themselves, saying:

21:26. If we shall say, from heaven, he will say to us: Why then did you not believe him? But if we shall say, from men, we are afraid of the multitude: for all held John as a prophet.

21:27. And answering Jesus, they said: We know not. He also said to them: Neither do I tell you by what authority I do these things.

21:28. But what think you? A certain man had two sons: and coming to the first, he said: Son, go work to day in my vineyard.

21:29. And he answering, said: I will not. But afterwards, being moved with repentance, he went.

21:30. And coming to the other, he said in like manner. And he answering said: I go, Sir. And he went not.

21:31. Which of the two did the father's will? They say to him: The first. Jesus saith to them: Amen I say to you that the publicans and the harlots shall go into the kingdom of God before you.

21:32. For John came to you in the way of justice: and you did not believe him. But the publicans and the harlots believed him: but you, seeing it, did not even afterwards repent, that you might believe him.

21:33. Hear ye another parable. There was a man, an householder, who planted a vineyard and made a hedge round about it and dug in it a press and built a tower and let it out to husbandmen and went into a strange country.

21:34. And when the time of the fruits drew nigh, he sent his servants to the husbandmen that they might receive the fruits thereof.

21:35. And the husbandmen laying hands on his servants, beat one and killed another and stoned another.

21:36. Again he sent other servants, more than the former; and they did to them in like manner.

21:37. And last of all he sent to them his son, saying: They will reverence my son.

21:38. But the husbandmen seeing the son, said among themselves: This is the heir: come, let us kill him, and we shall have his inheritance.

21:39. And taking him, they cast him forth out of the vineyard and killed him.

21:40. When therefore the lord of the vineyard shall come, what will he do to those husbandmen?

21:41. They say to him: He will bring those evil men to an evil end and let out his vineyard to other husbandmen that shall render him the fruit in due season.

21:42. Jesus saith to them: Have you never read in the Scriptures: The stone which the builders rejected, the same is become the head of the corner? By the Lord this has been done; and it is wonderful in our eyes.

21:43. Therefore I say to you that the kingdom of God shall be taken from you and shall be given to a nation yielding the fruits thereof.

21:44. And whosoever shall fall on this stone shall be broken: but on whomsoever it shall fall, it shall grind him to powder.

21:45. And when the chief priests and Pharisees had heard his parables, they knew that he spoke of them.

21:46. And seeking to lay hands on him, they feared the multitudes, because they held him as a prophet.

Chapter 22

The parable of the marriage feast. Christ orders tribute to be paid to Caesar. He confutes the Sadducees, shews which is the first commandment in the law and puzzles the Pharisees.

22:1. And Jesus answering, spoke again in parables to them, saying:

22:2. The kingdom of heaven is likened to a king who made a marriage for his son.
22:3. And he sent his servants to call them that were invited to the marriage: and they would not come.

22:4. Again he sent other servants, saying: Tell them that were invited, Behold, I have prepared my dinner: my beeves and fatlings are killed, and all things are ready. Come ye to the marriage.

22:5. But they neglected and went their ways, one to his farm and another to his merchandise.

22:6. And the rest laid hands on his servants and, having treated them contumeliously, put them to death.

22:7. But when the king had heard of it, he was angry: and sending his armies, he destroyed those murderers and burnt their city.

22:8. Then he saith to his servants: The marriage indeed is ready; but they that were invited were not worthy.

22:9. Go ye therefore into the highways; and as many as you shall find, call to the marriage.

22:10. And his servants going forth into the ways, gathered together all that they found, both bad and good: and the marriage was filled with guests.

22:11. And the king went in to see the guests: and he saw there a man who had not on a wedding garment.
22:12. And he saith to him: Friend, how camest thou in hither not having on a wedding garment? But he was silent.

22:13. Then the king said to the waiters: Bind his hands and feet, and cast him into the exterior darkness. There shall be weeping and gnashing of teeth.

22:14. For many are called, but few are chosen.

22:15. Then the Pharisees going, consulted among themselves how to insnare him in his speech.

22:16. And they sent to him their disciples with the Herodians, saying: Master, we know that thou art a true speaker and teachest the way of God in truth. Neither carest thou for any man: for thou dost not regard the person of men.

The Herodians... That is, some that belonged to Herod, and that joined with him in standing up for the necessity of paying tribute to Caesar, that is, to the Roman emperor. Some are of opinion that there was a sect among the Jews called Herodians, from their maintaining that Herod was the Messias.

22:17. Tell us therefore what dost thou think? Is it lawful to give tribute to Caesar, or not?

22:18. But Jesus knowing their wickedness, said: Why do you tempt me, ye hypocrites?

22:19. Shew me the coin of the tribute. And they offered him a penny.

22:20. And Jesus saith to them: Whose image and inscription is this?

22:21. They say to him: Caesar's. Then he saith to them: Render therefore to Caesar the things that are Caesar's; and to God, the things that are God's.

22:22. And hearing this, they wondered and, leaving him, went their ways.

22:23. That day there came to him the Sadducees, who say there is no resurrection; and asked him,

22:24. Saying: Master, Moses said: If a man die having no son, his brother shall marry his wife and raise up issue to his brother.

22:25. Now there were with us seven brethren: and the first having married a wife, died; and not having issue, left his wife to his brother.

22:26. In like manner the second and the third and so on, to the seventh.

22:27. And last of all the woman died also.

22:28. At the resurrection therefore, whose wife of the seven shall she be? For they all had her.

22:29. And Jesus answering, said to them: You err, not knowing the Scriptures nor the power of God.

22:30. For in the resurrection they shall neither

marry nor be married, but shall be as the angels of God in heaven.

22:31. And concerning the resurrection of the dead, have you not read that which was spoken by God, saying to you:

22:32. I am the God of Abraham and the God of Isaac and the God of Jacob? He is not the God of the dead but of the living.

22:33. And the multitudes hearing it were in admiration at his doctrine.

22:34. But the Pharisees, hearing that he had silenced the Sadducees, came together.

22:35. And one of them, a doctor of the law, asked him, tempting him:

22:36. Master, which is the great commandment in the law?

22:37. Jesus said to him: Thou shalt love the Lord thy God with thy whole heart and with thy whole soul and with thy whole mind.

22:38. This is the greatest and the first commandment.

22:39. And the second is like to this: Thou shalt love thy neighbour as thyself.

22:40. On these two commandments dependeth the whole law and the prophets.

22:41. And the Pharisees being gathered together, Jesus asked them,

22:42. Saying: What think you of Christ? Whose son is he? They say to him: David's.

22:43. He saith to them: How then doth David in spirit call him Lord, saying:

22:44. The Lord said to my Lord: Sit on my right hand, until I make thy enemies thy footstool?

22:45. If David then call him Lord, how is he his son?

22:46. And no man was able to answer him a word: neither durst any man from that day forth ask him any more questions.

Chapter 23

Christ admonishes the people to follow the good doctrine, not the bad example of the scribes and Pharisees. He warns his disciples not to imitate their ambition and denounces divers woes against them for their hypocrisy and blindness.

23:1. Then Jesus spoke to the multitudes and to his disciples,

23:2. Saying: The scribes and the Pharisees have sitten on the chair of Moses.

23:3. All things therefore whatsoever they shall

say to you, observe and do: but according to their works do ye not. For they say, and do not.

23:4. For they bind heavy and insupportable burdens and lay them on men's shoulders: but with a finger of their own they will not move them.

23:5. And all their works they do for to be seen of men. For they make their phylacteries broad and enlarge their fringes.

Phylacteries... that is, parchments, on which they wrote the ten commandments, and carried them on their foreheads before their eyes: which the Pharisees affected to wear broader than other men; so to seem more zealous for the law.

23:6. And they love the first places at feasts and the first chairs in the synagogues,

23:7. And salutations in the market place, and to be called by men, Rabbi.

23:8. But be not you called Rabbi. For one is your master: and all you are brethren.

23:9. And call none your father upon earth; for one is your father, who is in heaven.

Call none your father--Neither be ye called masters, etc... The meaning is that our Father in heaven is incomparably more to be regarded, than any father upon earth: and no master to be followed, who would lead us away from Christ. But this does not hinder but that we are by the law of

God to have a due respect both for our parents and spiritual fathers, (1 Cor. 4. 23:15,) and for our masters and teachers.

23:10. Neither be ye called masters: for one is your master, Christ.

23:11. He that is the greatest among you shall be your servant.

23:12. And whosoever shall exalt himself shall be humbled: and he that shall humble himself shall be exalted.

23:13. But woe to you, scribes and Pharisees, hypocrites, because you shut the kingdom of heaven against men: for you yourselves do not enter in and those that are going in, you suffer not to enter.

23:14. Woe to you scribes and Pharisees, hypocrites, because you devour the houses of widows, praying long prayers. For this you shall receive the greater judgment.

23:15. Woe to you, scribes and Pharisees, hypocrites, because you go round about the sea and the land to make one proselyte. And when he is made, you make him the child of hell twofold more than yourselves.

23:16. Woe to you, blind guides, that say, Whosoever shall swear by the temple, it is nothing; but he that shall swear by the gold of the temple is a debtor.

23:17. Ye foolish and blind: for whether is greater, the gold or the temple that sanctifieth the gold?

23:18. And whosoever shall swear by the altar, it is nothing; but whosoever shall swear by the gift that is upon it is a debtor.

23:19. Ye foolish and blind: for whether is greater, the gift or the altar that sanctifieth the gift?

23:20. He therefore that sweareth by the altar sweareth by it and by all things that are upon it.

23:21. And whosoever shall swear by the temple sweareth by it and by him that dwelleth in it.

23:22. And he that sweareth by heaven sweareth by the throne of God and by him that sitteth thereon.

23:23. Woe to you, scribes and Pharisees, hypocrites; because you tithe mint and anise and cummin and have left the weightier things of the law: judgment and mercy and faith. These things you ought to have done and not to leave those undone.

23:24. Blind guides, who strain out a gnat and swallow a camel.

23:25. Woe to you, scribes and Pharisees, hypocrites; because you make clean the outside of the cup and of the dish, but within you are full of rapine and uncleanness.

23:26. Thou blind Pharisee, first make clean the inside of the cup and of the dish, that the outside may become clean.

23:27. Woe to you, scribes and Pharisees, hypocrites; because you are like to whited sepulchres, which outwardly appear to men beautiful but within are full of dead men's bones and of all filthiness.

23:28. So you also outwardly indeed appear to men just: but inwardly you are full of hypocrisy and iniquity.

23:29. Woe to you, scribes and Pharisees, hypocrites, that build the sepulchres of the prophets and adorn the monuments of the just,

Build the sepulchres, etc... This is not blamed, as if it were in itself evil to build or adorn the monuments of the prophets: but the hypocrisy of the Pharisees is here taxed; who, whilst they pretended to honour the memory of the prophets, were persecuting even unto death the Lord of the prophets.

23:30. And say: If we had been in the days of our fathers, we would not have been partakers with them in the blood of the prophets.

23:31. Wherefore you are witnesses against yourselves, that you are the sons of them that killed the prophets.

23:32. Fill ye up then the measure of your fathers.

23:33. You serpents, generation of vipers, how will you flee from the judgment of hell?

23:34. Therefore behold I send to you prophets and wise men and scribes: and some of them you will put to death and crucify: and some you will scourge in your synagogues and persecute from city to city.

23:35. That upon you may come all the just blood that hath been shed upon the earth, from the blood of Abel the just, even unto the blood of Zacharias the son of Barachias, whom you killed between the temple and the altar.

That upon you may come, etc... Not that they should suffer more than their own sins justly deserved; but that the justice of God should now fall upon them with such a final vengeance, once for all, as might comprise all the different kinds of judgments and punishments, that had at any time before been inflicted for the shedding of just blood.

23:36. Amen I say to you, all these things shall come upon this generation.

23:37. Jerusalem, Jerusalem, thou that killest the prophets and stonest them that are sent unto thee, how often would I have gathered together thy children, as the hen doth gather her chickens under her wings, and thou wouldst not?

23:38. Behold, your house shall be left to you, desolate.

23:39. For I say to you, you shall not see me henceforth till you say: Blessed is he that cometh in the name of the Lord.

Chapter 24

Christ foretells the destruction of the temple, with the signs that shall come before it and before the last judgment. We must always watch.

24:1. And Jesus being come out of the temple, went away. And his disciples came to shew him the buildings of the temple.

24:2. And he answering, said to them: Do you see all these things? Amen I say to you, there shall not be left here a stone upon a stone that shall not be destroyed.

24:3. And when he was sitting on mount Olivet, the disciples came to him privately, saying: Tell us when shall these things be? And what shall be the sign of thy coming and of the consummation of the world?

24:4. And Jesus answering, said to them: Take heed that no man seduce you.

24:5. For many will come in my name saying, I am Christ. And they will seduce many.

24:6. And you shall hear of wars and rumours of

wars. See that ye be not troubled. For these things must come to pass: but the end is not yet.

24:7. For nation shall rise against nation, and kingdom against kingdom: And there shall be pestilences and famines and earthquakes in places.

24:8. Now all these are the beginnings of sorrows.

24:9. Then shall they deliver you up to be afflicted and shall put you to death: and you shall be hated by all nations for my name's sake.

24:10. And then shall many be scandalized and shall betray one another and shall hate one another.

24:11. And many false prophets shall rise and shall seduce many.

24:12. And because iniquity hath abounded, the charity of many shall grow cold.

24:13. But he that shall persevere to the end, he shall be saved.

24:14. And this gospel of the kingdom shall be preached in the whole world, for a testimony to all nations: and then shall the consummation come.

24:15. When therefore you shall see the abomination of desolation, which was spoken of by Daniel the prophet, standing in the holy place: he that readeth let him understand.

24:16. Then they that are in Judea, let them flee to the mountains:

24:17. And he that is on the housetop, let him not come down to take any thing out of his house:

24:18. And he that is in the field, let him not go back to take his coat.

24:19. And woe to them that are with child and that give suck in those days.

24:20. But pray that your flight be not in the winter or on the sabbath.

24:21. For there shall be then great tribulation, such as hath not been from the beginning of the world until now, neither shall be.

24:22. And unless those days had been shortened, no flesh should be saved: but for the sake of the elect those days shall be shortened.

24:23. Then if any man shall say to you, Lo here is Christ, or there: do not believe him.

24:24. For there shall arise false Christs and false prophets and shall shew great signs and wonders, insomuch as to deceive (if possible) even the elect.

24:25. Behold I have told it to you, beforehand.

24:26. If therefore they shall say to you, Behold he is in the desert: go ye not out. Behold he is in the closets: believe it not.

24:27. For as lightning cometh out of the east and appeareth even into the west: so shall also the cowling of the Son of man be.

24:28. Wheresoever the body shall be, there shall the eagles also be gathered together.

Wheresoever, etc... The coming of Christ shall be sudden, and manifest to all the world, like lightning: and wheresoever he shall come, thither shall all mankind be gathered to him, as eagles are gathered about a dead body.

24:29. And immediately after the tribulation of those days, the sun shall be darkened and the moon shall not give her light and the stars shall fall from heaven and the powers of heaven shall be moved.

The stars... Or flaming meteors resembling stars.

24:30. And then shall appear the sign of the Son of man in heaven. And then shall all tribes of the earth mourn: and they shall see the Son of man coming in the clouds of heaven with much power and majesty.

The sign, etc... The cross of Christ.

24:31. And he shall send his angels with a trumpet and a great voice: and they shall gather together his elect from the four winds, from the farthest parts of the heavens to the utmost bounds of them.

24:32. And from the fig tree learn a parable: When the branch thereof is now tender and the leaves come forth, you know that summer is nigh.

24:33. So you also, when you shall see all these things, know ye that it is nigh, even at the doors.

24:34. Amen I say to you that this generation shall not pass till all these things be done.

24:35. Heaven and earth shall pass: but my words shall not pass.

Shall pass... Because they shall be changed at the end of the world into a new heaven and new earth.

24:36. But of that day and hour no one knoweth: no, not the angels of heaven, but the Father alone.

24:37. And as in the days of Noe, so shall also the coming of the Son of man be.

24:38. For, as in the days before the flood they were eating and drinking, marrying and giving in marriage, even till that day in which Noe entered into the ark:

24:39. And they knew not till the flood came and took them all away: so also shall the coming of the Son of man be.

24:40. Then two shall be in the field. One shall be taken and one shall be left.

24:41. Two women shall be grinding at the mill. One shall be taken and one shall be left.

24:42. Watch ye therefore, because you know not what hour your Lord will come.

24:43. But this know ye, that, if the goodman of the house knew at what hour the thief would come, he would certainly watch and would not suffer his house to be broken open.

24:44. Wherefore be you also ready, because at what hour you know not the Son of man will come.

24:45. Who, thinkest thou, is a faithful and wise servant, whom his lord hath appointed over his family, to give them meat in season?

24:46. Blessed is that servant, whom when his lord shall come he shall find so doing.

24:47. Amen I say to you: he shall place him over all his goods.

24:48. But if that evil servant shall say in his heart: My lord is long a coming:

24:49. And shall begin to strike his fellow servants and shall eat and drink with drunkards:

24:50. The lord of that servant shall come in a day that he hopeth not and at an hour that he knoweth not:

24:51. And shall separate him and appoint his

portion with the hypocrites. There shall be weeping and gnashing of teeth.

Chapter 25

The parable of the ten virgins and of the talents. The description of the last judgment.

25:1. Then shall the kingdom of heaven be like to ten virgins, who taking their lamps went out to meet the bridegroom and the bride.

25:2. And five of them were foolish and five wise.

25:3. But the five foolish, having taken their lamps, did not take oil with them.

25:4. But the wise took oil in their vessels with the lamps.

25:5. And the bridegroom tarrying, they all slumbered and slept.

25:6. And at midnight there was a cry made: Behold the bridegroom cometh. Go ye forth to meet him.

25:7. Then all those virgins arose and trimmed their lamps.

25:8. And the foolish said to the wise: Give us of your oil, for our lamps are gone out.

25:9. The wise answered, saying: Lest perhaps

there be not enough for us and for you, go ye rather to them that sell and buy for yourselves.

25:10. Now whilst they went to buy the bridegroom came: and they that were ready went in with him to the marriage. And the door was shut.

25:11. But at last came also the other virgins, saying: Lord, Lord, open to us.

25:12. But he answering said: Amen I say to you, I know you not.

25:13. Watch ye therefore, because you know not the day nor the hour.

25:14. For even as a man going into a far country called his servants and delivered to them his goods;

25:15. And to one he gave five talents, and to another two, and to another one, to every one according to his proper ability: and immediately he took his journey.

25:16. And he that had received the five talents went his way and traded with the same and gained other five.

25:17. And in like manner he that had received the two gained other two.

25:18. But he that had received the one, going his way, digged into the earth and hid his lord's money.

25:19. But after a long time the lord of those servants came and reckoned with them.

25:20. And he that had received the five talents coming, brought other five talents, saying: Lord, thou didst deliver to me five talents. Behold I have gained other five over and above.

25:21. His lord said to him: Well done, good and faithful servant, because thou hast been faithful over a few things, I will place thee over many things. Enter thou into the joy of thy lord.

25:22. And he also that had received the two talents came and said: Lord, thou deliveredst two talents to me. Behold I have gained other two.

25:23. His lord said to him: Well done, good and faithful servant: because thou hast been faithful over a few things, I will place thee over many things. Enter thou into the joy of thy lord.

25:24. But he that had received the one talent, came and said: Lord, I know that thou art a hard man; thou reapest where thou hast not sown and gatherest where thou hast not strewed.

25:25. And being afraid, I went and hid thy talent in the earth. Behold here thou hast that which is thine.

25:26. And his lord answering, said to him: Wicked and slothful servant, thou knewest that I reap where I sow not and gather where I have not strewed.

25:27. Thou oughtest therefore to have committed my money to the bankers: and at my coming I should have received my own with usury.

25:28. Take ye away therefore the talent from him and give it him that hath ten talents.

25:29. For to every one that hath shall be given, and he shall abound: but from him that hath not, that also which he seemeth to have shall be taken away.

25:30. And the unprofitable servant, cast ye out into the exterior darkness. There shall be weeping and gnashing of teeth.

25:31. And when the Son of man shall come in his majesty, and all the angels with him, then shall he sit upon the seat of his majesty.

25:32. And all nations shall be gathered together before him: and he shall separate them one from another, as the shepherd separateth the sheep from the goats:

25:33. And he shall set the sheep on his right hand, but the goats on his left.

25:34. Then shall the king say to them that shall be on his right hand: Come, ye blessed of my Father, possess you the kingdom prepared for you from the foundation of the world.

25:35. For I was hungry, and you gave me to eat: I was thirsty, and you gave me to drink: I was a stranger, and you took me in:

25:36. Naked, and you covered me: sick, and you visited me: I was in prison, and you came to me.

25:37. Then shall the just answer him, saying: Lord, when did we see thee hungry and fed thee: thirsty and gave thee drink?

25:38. Or when did we see thee a stranger and took thee in? Or naked and covered thee?

25:39. Or when did we see thee sick or in prison and came to thee?

25:40. And the king answering shall say to them: Amen I say to you, as long as you did it to one of these my least brethren, you did it to me.

25:41. Then he shall say to them also that shall be on his left hand: Depart from me, you cursed, into everlasting fire, which was prepared for the devil and his angels.

25:42. For I was hungry and you gave me not to eat: I was thirsty and you gave me not to drink.

25:43. I was a stranger and you took me not in: naked and you covered me not: sick and in prison and you did not visit me.

25:44. Then they also shall answer him, saying:

Lord, when did we see thee hungry or thirsty or a stranger or naked or sick or in prison and did not minister to thee?

25:45. Then he shall answer them, saying: Amen: I say to you, as long as you did it not to one of these least, neither did you do it to me.

25:46. And these shall go into everlasting punishment: but the just, into life everlasting.

Chapter 26

The Jews conspire against Christ. He is anointed by Mary. The treason of Judas. The last supper. The prayer in the garden. The apprehension of our Lord. His treatment in the house of Caiphas.

26:1. And it came to pass, when Jesus had ended all these words, he said to his disciples:

26:2. You know that after two days shall be the pasch: and the Son of man shall be delivered up to be crucified.

26:3. Then were gathered together the chief priests and ancients of the people, into the court of the high priest, who was called Caiphas:

26:4. And they consulted together that by subtilty they might apprehend Jesus and put him to death.

26:5. But they said: Not on the festival day, lest perhaps there should be a tumult among the people.

26:6. And when Jesus was in Bethania, in the house of Simon the leper,

26:7. There came to him a woman having an alabaster box of precious ointment and poured it on his head as he was at table.

26:8. And the disciples seeing it had indignation, saying: To what purpose is this waste?

26:9. For this might have been sold for much and given to the poor.

26:10. And Jesus knowing it, said to them: Why do you trouble this woman? For she hath wrought a good work upon me.

26:11. For the poor you have always with you: but me you have not always.

Me you have not always... Viz., in a visible manner, as when conversant here on earth; and as we have the poor, whom we may daily assist and relieve.

26:12. For she in pouring this ointment on my body hath done it for my burial.

26:13. Amen I say to you, wheresoever this gospel shall be preached in the whole world, that also which she hath done shall be told for a memory of her.

26:14. Then went one of the twelve, who was called Judas Iscariot, to the chief priests.

26:15. And said to them: What will you give me, and I will deliver him unto you? But they appointed him thirty pieces of silver.

26:16. And from thenceforth he sought opportunity to betray him.

26:17. And on the first day of the Azymes, the disciples came to Jesus, saying: Where wilt thou that we prepare for thee to eat the pasch?

Azymes... Feast of the unleavened bread. Pasch... The paschal lamb.

26:18. But Jesus said: Go ye into the city to a certain man and say to him: The master saith, My time is near at hand. With thee I make the pasch with my disciples.

26:19. And the disciples did as Jesus appointed to them: and they prepared the pasch.

26:20. But when it was evening, he sat down with his twelve disciples.

26:21. And whilst they were eating, he said: Amen I say to you that one of you is about to betray me.

26:22. And they being very much troubled began every one to say: Is it I, Lord?

26:23. But he answering said: He that dippeth his hand with me in the dish, he shall betray me.

26:24. The Son of man indeed goeth, as it is written of him. But woe to that man by whom the Son of man shall be betrayed. It were better for him, if that man had not been born.

26:25. And Judas that betrayed him answering, said: Is it I, Rabbi? He saith to him: Thou hast said it.

26:26. And whilst they were at supper, Jesus took bread and blessed and broke and gave to his disciples and said: Take ye and eat. This is my body.

This is my body... He does not say, This is the figure of my body--but This is my body. (2 Council of Nice, Act. 6.) Neither does he say in this, or with this is my body; but absolutely, This is my body: which plainly implies transubstantiation.

26:27. And taking the chalice, he gave thanks and gave to them, saying: Drink ye all of this.

Drink ye all of this... This was spoken to the twelve apostles; who were the all then present; and they all drank of it, says St. Mark 14. 23. But it no ways follows from these words spoken to the apostles, that all the faithful are here commanded to drink of the chalice; any more than that all the faithful are commanded to consecrate, offer and administer this sacrament; because Christ upon this same occasion, and at the same time, bid the apostles do so; in these words, St. Luke 22. 19, Do this for a commemoration of me.

26:28. For this is my blood of the new testament, which shall be shed for many unto remission of sins.

Blood of the new testament... As the old testament was dedicated with the blood of victims, by Moses, in these words: This is the blood of the testament, etc., Heb. 9. 20; so here is the dedication and institution of the new testament, in the blood of Christ, here mystically shed by these words: This is the blood of the new testament, etc.

26:29. And I say to you, I will not drink from henceforth of this fruit of the vine until that day when I shall drink it with you new in the kingdom of my Father.

Fruit of the vine... These words, by the account of St. Luke 26:22. 18, were not spoken of the sacramental cup, but of the wine that was drunk with the paschal lamb. Though the sacramental cup might also be called the fruit of the vine, because it was consecrated from wine, and retains the likeness, and all the accidents or qualities of wine.

26:30. And a hymn being said, they went out unto mount Olivet.

26:31. Then Jesus saith to them: All you shall be scandalized in me this night. For it is written: I will strike the shepherd: and the sheep of the flock shall be dispersed.

Scandalized in me, etc... Forasmuch as my being apprehended shall make you all run away and forsake me.

26:32. But after I shall be risen again, I will go before you into Galilee.

26:33. And Peter answering, said to him: Although all shall be scandalized in thee, I will never be scandalized.

26:34. Jesus said to him: Amen I say to thee that in this night before the cock crow, thou wilt deny me thrice.

26:35. Peter saith to him: Yea, though I should die with thee, I will not deny thee. And in like manner said all the disciples.

26:36. Then Jesus came with them into a country place which is called Gethsemani. And he said to his disciples: Sit you here, till I go yonder and pray.

26:37. And taking with him Peter and the two sons of Zebedee, he began to grow sorrowful and to be sad.

26:38. Then he saith to them: My soul is sorrowful even unto death. Stay you here and watch with me.

26:39. And going a little further, he fell upon his face, praying and saying: My Father, if it be possible, let this chalice pass from me. Nevertheless, not as I will but as thou wilt.

26:40. And he cometh to his disciples and findeth them asleep. And he saith to Peter: What? Could you not watch one hour with me?

26:41. Watch ye: and pray that ye enter not into temptation. The spirit indeed is willing, but the flesh is weak.

26:42. Again the second time, he went and prayed, saying: My Father, if this chalice may not pass away, but I must drink it, thy will be done.

26:43. And he cometh again and findeth them sleeping: for their eyes were heavy.

26:44. And leaving them, he went again: and he prayed the third time, saying the selfsame word.

26:45. Then he cometh to his disciples and said to them: Sleep ye now and take your rest. Behold the hour is at hand: and the Son of man shall be betrayed into the hands of sinners.

26:46. Rise: let us go. Behold he is at hand that will betray me.

26:47. As he yet spoke, behold Judas, one of the twelve, came, and with him a great multitude with swords and clubs, sent from the chief priests and the ancients of the people.

26:48. And he that betrayed him gave them a

sign, saying: Whomsoever I shall kiss, that is he. Hold him fast.

26:49. And forthwith coming to Jesus, he said: Hail, Rabbi. And he kissed him.

26:50. And Jesus said to him: Friend, whereto art thou come? Then they came up and laid hands on Jesus and held him.

26:51. And behold one of them that were with Jesus, stretching forth his hand, drew out his sword: and striking the servant of the high priest, cut off his ear.

26:52. Then Jesus saith to him: Put up again thy sword into its place: for all that take the sword shall perish with the sword.

26:53. Thinkest thou that I cannot ask my Father, and he will give me presently more than twelve legions of angels?

26:54. How then shall the scriptures be fulfilled, that so it must be done?

26:55. In that same hour, Jesus said to the multitudes: You are come out, as it were to a robber, with swords and clubs to apprehend me. I sat daily with you, teaching in the temple: and you laid not hands on me.

26:56. Now all this was done that the scriptures of the prophets might be fulfilled. Then the disciples, all leaving him, fled.

26:57. But they holding Jesus led him to Caiphas the high priest, where the scribes and the ancients were assembled.

26:58. And Peter followed him afar off, even to the court of the high priest, And going in, he sat with the servants, that he might see the end.

26:59. And the chief priests and the whole council sought false witness against Jesus, that they might put him to death.

26:60. And they found not, whereas many false witnesses had come in. And last of all there came two false witnesses:

26:61. And they said: This man said, I am able to destroy the temple of God and after three days to rebuild it.

26:62. And the high priest rising up, said to him: Answerest thou nothing to the things which these witness against thee?

26:63. But Jesus held his peace. And the high priest said to him: I adjure thee by the living God, that thou tell us if thou be the Christ the Son of God.

26:64. Jesus saith to him: Thou hast said it. Nevertheless I say to you, hereafter you shall see the Son of man sitting on the right hand of the power of God and coming in the clouds of heaven.

26:65. Then the high priest rent his garments, saying: He hath blasphemed: What further need have we of witnesses? Behold, now you have heard the blasphemy.

26:66. What think you? But they answering, said: He is guilty of death.

26:67. Then did they spit in his face and buffeted him. And others struck his face with the palms of their hands,

26:68. Saying: Prophesy unto us, O Christ. Who is he that struck thee?

26:69. But Peter sat without in the court. And there came to him a servant maid, saying: Thou also wast with Jesus the Galilean.

26:70. But he denied before them all, saying: I know not what thou sayest.

26:71. And as he went out of the gate, another maid saw him; and she saith to them that were there: This man also was with Jesus of Nazareth.

26:72. And again he denied with an oath: I know not the man.

26:73. And after a little while, they came that stood by and said to Peter: Surely thou also art one of them. For even thy speech doth discover thee.

26:74. Then he began to curse and to swear that he knew not the man. And immediately the cock crew.

26:75. And Peter remembered the word of Jesus which he had said: Before the cock crow, thou wilt deny me thrice. And going forth, he wept bitterly.

Chapter 27

The continuation of the history of the passion of Christ. His death and burial.

27:1. And when morning was come, all the chief priests and ancients of the people took counsel against Jesus, that they might put him to death.

27:2. And they brought him bound and delivered him to Pontius Pilate the governor.

27:3. Then Judas, who betrayed him, seeing that he was condemned, repenting himself, brought back the thirty pieces of silver to the chief priests and ancients,

27:4. Saying: I have sinned in betraying innocent blood. But they said: What is that to us? Look thou to it.

27:5. And casting down the pieces of silver in the temple, he departed and went and hanged himself with an halter.

27:6. But the chief priests having taken the pieces of silver, said: It is not lawful to put them into the corbona, because it is the price of blood.

Corbona... A place in the temple where the people put in their gifts or offerings.

27:7. And after they had consulted together, they bought with them the potter's field, to be a burying place for strangers.

27:8. For this cause that field was called Haceldama, that is, the field of blood, even to this day.

27:9. Then was fulfilled that which was spoken by Jeremias the prophet, saying: And they took the thirty pieces of silver, the price of him that was prized, whom they prized of the children of Israel.

27:10. And they gave them unto the potter's field, as the Lord appointed to me.

27:11. And Jesus stood before the governor, and the governor asked him, saying: Art thou the king of the Jews? Jesus saith to him: Thou sayest it.

27:12. And when he was accused by the chief priests and ancients, he answered nothing.

27:13. Then Pilate saith to him: Dost not thou hear how great testimonies they allege against thee?

27:14. And he answered him to never a word, so that the governor wondered exceedingly.

27:15. Now upon the solemn day the governor was accustomed to release to the people one prisoner, whom they would.

27:16. And he had then a notorious prisoner that was called Barabbas.

27:17. They therefore being gathered together, Pilate said: Whom will you that I release to You: Barabbas, or Jesus that is called Christ?

27:18. For he knew that for envy they had delivered him.

27:19. And as he was sitting in the place of judgment, his wife sent to him, saying: Have thou nothing to do with that just man; for I have suffered many things this day in a dream because of him.

27:20. But the chief priests and ancients persuaded the people that they should ask Barabbas and make Jesus away.

27:21. And the governor answering, said to them: Whether will you of the two to be released unto you? But they said: Barabbas.

27:22. Pilate saith to them: What shall I do then with Jesus that is called Christ? They say all: Let him be crucified.

27:23. The governor said to them: Why, what evil hath he done? But they cried out the more, saying: Let him be crucified.

27:24. And Pilate seeing that he prevailed nothing, but that rather a tumult was made, taking water washed his hands before the people, saying:

I am innocent of the blood of this just man. Look you to it.

27:25. And the whole people answering, said: His blood be upon us and upon our children.

27:26. Then he released to them Barabbas: and having scourged Jesus, delivered him unto them to be crucified.

27:27. Then the soldiers of the governor, taking Jesus into the hall, gathered together unto him the whole band.

27:28. And stripping him, they put a scarlet cloak about him.

27:29. And platting a crown of thorns, they put it upon his head, and a reed in his right hand. And bowing the knee before him, they mocked him, saying: Hail, King of the Jews.

27:30. And spitting upon him, they took the reed and struck his head.

27:31. And after they had mocked him, they took off the cloak from him and put on him his own garments and led him away to crucify him.

27:32. And going out, they found a man of Cyrene, named Simon: him they forced to take up his cross.

27:33. And they came to the place that is called Golgotha, which is the place of Calvary.

27:34. And they gave him wine to drink mingled with gall. And when he had tasted, he would not drink.

27:35. And after they had crucified him, they divided his garments, casting lots; that it might be fulfilled which was spoken by the prophet, saying: They divided my garments among them; and upon my vesture they cast lots.

27:36. And they sat and watched him.

27:37. And they put over his head his cause written: THIS IS JESUS THE KING OF THE JEWS.

27:38. Then were crucified with him two thieves: one on the right hand and one on the left.

27:39. And they that passed by blasphemed him, wagging their heads,

27:40. And saying: Vah, thou that destroyest the temple of God and in three days dost rebuild it: save thy own self. If thou be the Son of God, come down from the cross.

27:41. In like manner also the chief priests, with the scribes and ancients, mocking said:

27:42. He saved others: himself he cannot save. If he be the king of Israel, let him now come down from the cross: and we will believe him.

27:43. He trusted in God: let him now deliver

him if he will have him. For he said: I am the Son of God.

27:44. And the selfsame thing the thieves also that were crucified with him reproached him with.

27:45. Now from the sixth hour, there was darkness over the whole earth, until the ninth hour.

27:46. And about the ninth hour, Jesus cried with a loud voice, saying: Eli, Eli, lamma sabacthani? That is, My God, My God, why hast thou forsaken me?

27:47. And some that stood there and heard said: This man calleth Elias.

27:48. And immediately one of them running took a sponge and filled it with vinegar and put it on a reed and gave him to drink.

27:49. And the others said: Let be. Let us see whether Elias will come to deliver him.

27:50. And Jesus again crying with a loud voice, yielded up the ghost.

27:51. And behold the veil of the temple was rent in two from the top even to the bottom: and the earth quaked and the rocks were rent.

27:52. And the graves were opened: and many bodies of the saints that had slept arose,

27:53. And coming out of the tombs after his

resurrection, came into the holy city and appeared to many.

27:54. Now the centurion and they that were with him watching Jesus, having seen the earthquake and the things that were done, were sore afraid, saying: Indeed this was the Son of God.

27:55. And there were there many women afar off, who had followed Jesus from Galilee, ministering unto him:

27:56. Among whom was Mary Magdalen and Mary the mother of James and Joseph and the mother of the sons of Zebedee.

27:57. And when it was evening, there came a certain rich man of Arimathea, named Joseph, who also himself was a disciple of Jesus.

27:58. He went to Pilate and asked the body of Jesus. Then Pilate commanded that the body should be delivered.

27:59. And Joseph taking the body wrapped it up in a clean linen cloth:

27:60. And laid it in his own new monument, which he had hewed out in a rock. And he rolled a great stone to the door of the monument and went his way.

27:61. And there was there Mary Magdalen and the other Mary, sitting over against the sepulchre.

27:62. And the next day, which followed the day of preparation, the chief priests and the Pharisees came together to Pilate,

The day of preparation... The eve of the sabbath; so called, because on that day they prepared all things necessary; not being allowed so much as to dress their meat on the sabbath day.

27:63. Saying: Sir, we have remembered, that that seducer said, while he was yet alive: After three days I will rise again.

27:64. Command therefore the sepulchre to be guarded until the third day: lest perhaps his disciples come and steal him away and say to the people: He is risen from the dead. And the last error shall be worse than the first.

27:65. Pilate saith to them: You have a guard. Go, guard it as you know.

27:66. And they departing, made the sepulchre sure, sealing the stone and setting guards.

Chapter 28

The resurrection of Christ. His commission to his disciples.

28:1. And in the end of the sabbath, when it began to dawn towards the first day of the week, came Mary Magdalen and the other Mary, to see the sepulchre.

28:2. And behold there was a great earthquake. For an angel of the Lord descended from heaven and coming rolled back the stone and sat upon it.

28:3. And his countenance was as lightning and his raiment as snow.

28:4. And for fear of him, the guards were struck with terror and became as dead men.

28:5. And the angel answering, said to the women: Fear not you: for I know that you seek Jesus who was crucified.

28:6. He is not here. For he is risen, as he said. Come, and see the place where the Lord was laid.

28:7. And going quickly, tell ye his disciples that he is risen. And behold he will go before you into Galilee. There you shall see him. Lo, I have foretold it to you.

28:8. And they went out quickly from the sepulchre with fear and great joy, running to tell his disciples.

28:9. And behold, Jesus met them, saying: All hail. But they came up and took hold of his feet and adored him.

28:10. Then Jesus said to them: Fear not. Go, tell my brethren that they go into Galilee. There they shall see me.

28:11. Who when they were departed, behold,

some of the guards came into the city and told the chief priests all things that had been done.

28:12. And they being assembled together with the ancients, taking counsel, gave a great sum of money to the soldiers,

28:13. Saying: Say you, His disciples came by night and stole him away when we were asleep.

28:14. And if the governor shall hear of this, we will persuade him and secure you.

28:15. So they taking the money, did as they were taught: and this word was spread abroad among the Jews even unto this day.

28:16. And the eleven disciples went into Galilee, unto the mountain where Jesus had appointed them.

28:17. And seeing him they adored: but some doubted.

28:18. And Jesus coming, spoke to them, saying: All power is given to me in heaven and in earth.

All power, etc... See here the warrant and commission of the apostles and their successors, the bishops and pastors of Christ's church. He received from his Father all power in heaven and in earth: and in virtue of this power, he sends them (even as his Father sent him, St. John 20. 21) to teach and disciple, not one, but all nations; and instruct them in all truths: and that he may assist them effectually in the execution of this commission, he promises to be with them, not for three or four hundred years only, but all days, even to the consummation of the world.

How then could the Catholic Church ever go astray; having always with her pastors, as is here promised, Christ himself, who is the way, the truth, and the life. St. John 14.

28:19. Going therefore, teach ye all nations: baptizing them in the name of the Father and of the Son and of the Holy Ghost.

28:20. Teaching them to observe all things whatsoever I have commanded you. And behold I am with you all days, even to the consummation of the world.

www.ingramcontent.com/pod-product-compliance
Lightning Source LLC
Chambersburg PA
CBHW060937040426
42445CB00011B/906